Counter Terrorism and Social Cohesion

Counter Terrorism and Social Cohesion

Edited by

Alperhan Babacan and Hussein Tahiri

CAMBRIDGE SCHOLARS

PUBLISHING

Counter Terrorism and Social Cohesion,
Edited by Alperhan Babacan and Hussein Tahiri

This book first published 2011

Cambridge Scholars Publishing

12 Back Chapman Street, Newcastle upon Tyne, NE6 2XX, UK

British Library Cataloguing in Publication Data
A catalogue record for this book is available from the British Library

ISBN (10): 1-4438-3292-8, ISBN (13): 978-1-4438-3292-2

CONTENTS

Chapter One 1
Mapping the Link between Counter Terrorism and Social Cohesion
Alperhan Babacan and Hussein Tahiri

Chapter Two 7
The International Regulation of Transnational Criminal Law
Donald Feaver

Chapter Three 27
Australia's Response to the War on Terror: A Preventative and Disproportionate Approach at the Cost of Human Rights Protections
Alperhan Babacan

Chapter Four 41
The Rising Politics of "Emergencies" in the Global Age: A Critical Reflection on the Governance of (In)Security in Australia
Selver B. Sahin

Chapter Five 61
Australia's War on Terrorism: Impact on Australian Muslim Communities
Tahmina Rashid

Chapter Six 81
War on Terror and Social Cohesion: National Security Discourse, Social Identity and Community Order
Robin Cameron

Chapter Seven 99
Creating Belonging: Safety, Racism and Social Cohesion
Hurriyet Babacan

Chapter Eight 117
Countering Terrorism through Community Engagement
Hussein Tahiri

Chapter Nine 135
Searching for Alternative Solutions
Hussein Tahiri and Alperhan Babacan

Editors and Contributors 141

CHAPTER ONE

MAPPING THE LINK BETWEEN COUNTER TERRORISM AND SOCIAL COHESION

ALPERHAN BABACAN AND HUSSEIN TAHIRI

Around the globe, the "war on terror" has been depicted as one that constitutes a "new threat", a war with unseen enemies, justifying the implementation of some exceptional measures to counter the "new threat" (Zedner 2005). In Australia, the advent of "globalised terrorism" in the wake of September 11 has resulted in the adoption of a so-called preventative approach to counter terrorism through the introduction of a raft of new counter-terrorism laws (Pickering, McCulloch and Wright-Neville 2007; Lynch and Williams 2006; Syrota 2008). These laws have created new criminal offences and provided extensive investigative, detention and questioning powers to security agencies and the police (Pickering and McCulloch 2010). The new legislative provisions are unprecedented in Australia's legal history and have led to claims that they infringe upon rights and liberties which are embedded in the Australian legal system and enshrined in international human rights law (Bronnit 2004, 2010). This book critically examines Australia's counter terrorism measures by looking at Australia's legislative framework, the Australian Government's justifications for the war on terrorism and sociological theories relating to "risk society" as a way to explain Australia's counter terrorism policies and the impact of the war on terror on social cohesion in Australia.

Formulating and implementing counter-terrorism laws is usually regarded as a national responsibility. However, sitting behind the majority of national counter-terror laws is an international framework of norms and institutions that are more comprehensive than is generally understood. Dr Feaver's chapter broadly describes this international institutional framework and identifies the principle norms relating to the global regulation of counter terrorism. Dr Feaver explains how international initiatives to regulate counter terrorism are unique in several respects. The chapter explains how, in response to the events of September 11, a significant development in international rule-making by the United Nations occurred. Dr Feaver also discusses how specialist UN agencies such as the UN Office of Drugs and Crimes (UNODC) and its Terrorism Prevention Branch (TPB) play an important norm harmonisation and monitoring role. Finally, he explains how the substantive character of international counter-terrorism norms represent a significant departure from the traditional conceptualisations of the functions of international law.

Dr Babacan's chapter critically examines the Australian Government's justifications for the war on terror and in particular its suspension of human rights and due process protections with respect to terrorism-related offences. After providing an overview of Australia's justification for the war on terror and Australia's counter terrorism regime, Dr Babacan argues that although the threat of terrorism is legitimate, the Australian Government has failed to publicly justify the exact nature and in particular the extent of the threat of terrorist attacks. It is argued that the legislative response to terrorism in Australia has been influenced by international pressure and with a disregard for its potential human rights implications rather than an actuarial examination of the cost-benefit balance normally involved in the legislation-making process. Dr Babacan argues that the net effect of Australia's counter-terrorism measures is profound and adversely impacts on human rights, civil liberties and notions of belonging. He advocates the reinstatement of key due processes and human rights protections.

While the risk of terrorism is real, the concept of security is a political construct (Beck 2006; Angamben 2005). The changes brought about by September 11 may be understood as part of the large-scale changes in the social control of societies which have emerged as a result of the growth of the "risk society" (Beck 2006; Ericson and Haggerty 1997; Goldsmith 2008). In Chapter 4, Dr Sahin critically examines the growing application of the concept of "emergencies" to the global politics of (in)security and its reflections on the conception of security in Australia. Drawing upon Beck's analysis of "world risk society" and Agamben's formulation of Schmitt's theory of "the state of exception as a dominant paradigm of governance", she examines the limits and contradictions of the contemporary policies and practices of the governance of security. Dr Sahin argues that the contemporary politics of "emergencies" not only tend to perpetuate the dynamics of political intervention as a form of government through the construction of fear of the enemy but also provide a powerful discursive escape from responsibility for the policies and practices that are themselves likely to create new "emergencies".

The war on terror has changed the social relations between mainstream Australians and Muslims. An important driver in the justification of the war on terror both internationally and on the home front has been the emphasis placed upon making a distinction between friends and enemies. Domestic issues relating to minorities, social cohesion and belonging have been reconfigured to justify Australia's commitment to the war on terror abroad and its commitment to curbing terrorism and terrorist-related activities. The discourses surrounding the justification for the war on terror and the counter-terrorism measures in Australia have resulted in the negative portrayal of Muslims and have adversely impacted on their sense of belonging in Australia and on social cohesion and community harmony (Poynting and Noble). In turn, discourses relating to the war on terror have legitimised a fear of difference, both the differences of some people living among us and the differences of some people who are entering the country, such as asylum seekers (Babacan, Gopalkrishnan and Babacan 2009; Williams 2003).

Chapters 5, 6 and 7 look at the adverse impacts of the war on terror on Muslims in Australia and their sense of belonging in a multicultural society, and analyse these developments from a sociological perspective.

Dr Rashid critically examines the impact of the war on terror on Muslims in Australia. She argues that the debates and legislation since 2001 around the themes of "counter terrorism", "war against terrorism" and "war on terrorism" in Australia have generated complex scenarios leading to fear and the creation of Otherness – "us versus them". Mainstream debates on counter terrorism have created fear of Muslims as the threat in mainstream society, and fear of the state among Muslims. Muslim communities have felt criminalised through legislation which overtly doubts their allegiance to Australia and suspects criminal intent. Public discourses have given an impression to Muslim communities that Muslims have the sole responsibility for countering terrorism in Australia and must provide information on potential suspects and suspicious activities in their communities. Muslims, especially of Middle Eastern origin, have become a "fifth column". Pakistani and Indian Muslims were also eventually labelled as terrorists – in dire need of scrutiny by all. Some of these negative discourses and legislative measures have created an atmosphere of "guilty by association", justifying curtailing civil liberties in the name of countering terrorism. Civil liberties advocates have criticised these measures as potential tools for victimisation on a number of political grounds. Muslim communities have of course experienced victimisation since these discourses entered public debate. Irrespective of the reality of these fears, Muslims are feeling the impact on their sense of belonging and their Australian identity because of being labelled as potential terrorists, guilty by association, un-Australian, Other, citizens with suspect allegiance and guilty until proven innocent. Muslim women at the same time have to confront an additional factor of negative perception if they choose to wear headscarves.

The chapters by Dr Cameron and Professor Babacan examine the effects of the war on terror on social cohesion through the shaping of social stereotypes and group identity. Dr Cameron argues that the war on terror – whether at home or abroad – invokes stark contrasts between friend and enemy, which both corresponds with and reinforces particular domestic social stereotypes. Dr Cameron argues that these stereotypes are complex in that they are not drawn solely from a domestic context but are also informed by Australia's participation in the global war on terror. The conflation of international conflicts and foreign threat into local community relations exacerbates existing social divisions as certain identities become associated with threats to national security.

In Chapter 7, Professor Babacan argues that the recent public discourses in Australia about social inclusion have taken place without regard to social exclusion based on ethnicity, religion and "race". Major events in recent Australian history that have been a cause for concern include racially motivated violence against Muslim communities, the Cronulla riots, attacks on international students, the vilification of asylum seekers and refugees, and other acts of racism. Professor Babacan argues in this chapter that social exclusion in Australia is articulated without denouncing democratic principles and through transformation into more palatable concerns. Coded societal messages are perpetuated through public discourses on the war on terror, immigration, multiculturalism, refugees and citizenship. The chapter concludes with an exploration of how social cohesion can be achieved – namely, through reclaiming critical multiculturalism and participation, and engendering a sense of equal valued status.

In Chapter 8, Dr Tahiri discusses countering terrorism through a community engagement strategy. Dr Tahiri argues that because the underlying causes of terrorism are multi-faceted and complex, a range of strategies needs to be employed in reducing the threat of terrorism. He argues that the state's resort to coercive powers has proven to be unsuccessful in combating terrorism and that the root causes of terrorism and the processes of radicalisation need to be addressed through community engagement. Discussing developments in Australia and particularly in the state of Victoria, Dr Tahiri provides a framework for engaging communities in the fight against terrorism and advocates for a comprehensive community engagement strategy that involves not only Muslim communities but also the community at large.

The final chapter draws broad conclusions about the war on terror, Australia's policies and their impact on Muslims in Australia, and the way forward in combating terrorism. It is argued that forcefully combating terrorism does not inhibit states from adhering to due process protections and the rule of law. Counter terrorism measures need to respect civil liberties and due process protections, and contemporary socio-cultural anxieties need to be addressed constructively. Counter terrorism measures need to address radicalism, stereotypes and the loss of social inclusion brought about by the war on terror. Terrorism arises from complex and multifaceted factors and counter strategies need to address such factors. The traditional "top-down", "paramilitary" and "coercive" approaches to tackling terrorism are not effective to combat radicalisation and extremism. A community engagement approach which encompasses all sectors of the community and government clearly is the way forward to combat terrorism and extremism. Such an approach will also in turn enhance social inclusion, participation, trust and respect. It is only through valuing cultural difference, inclusion and fostering a sense of belonging that social inclusion will be strengthened.

References

Agamben, G. 2005. *The state of exception*, trans. Kevin Attell. Chicago, London: The University of Chicago Press.

Babacan H., N. Gopalkrishnan and A. Babacan. 2009. *Situating racism: The local, national, and the global.* Cambridge: Cambridge Scholars Press.

Beck U. 2006. Living in the world risk society. *Economy and Society* 35 (3): 329–345.

Bronitt, S. 2004. Australia's legal response to terrorism: Neither novel nor extraordinary. In *Human rights 2003: The year in review*, ed. T. Davis. Clayton: Monash University.

—. 2010. Preface. In *Dealing with uncertainties in policing serious crime*, ed. G. Bammer. Canberra: ANU E Press.

Ericson, R. and K. Haggerty. 1997. *Policing the risk*. Oxford: Clarendon.

Goldsmith, A. 2008. The governance of terror: Precautionary logic and counter-terrorist law reform after September 11. *Law and Policy* 30 (2): 142–167.

Lynch, A. and G. Williams. 2006. What price security? Taking stock of Australia's anti-terror laws. Sydney: UNSW Press.

Pickering, S. and J. McCulloch. 2010. The Haneef case and counter terrorism policing in Australia. *Policing and Society* 20 (1): 21–38.

Pickering, S., D. Wright-Neville, J. McCulloch and P. Lentini. 2007. *Counter-terrorism policing and culturally diverse communities: Final report*. Clayton: Monash University.

Poynting. S and G. Noble. 2004. Living with racism: The experience and reporting by Arab and Muslim Australians of discrimination, abuse and violence since September 2001. Report to the Human Rights and Equal Opportunity Commission, 19 April 2004, www.hreoc.gov.au/racial_discrimination/isma/research/index.html (accessed 10 November 2010).

Syrota, G. 2008. Australia's counter terrorism offences: A critical study. *University of Western Australia Law Review* 34: 103–144.

Williams, M. C. 2003. Words, images, enemies: Securitization and international politics. *International Studies Quarterly* 47 (4): 511–531.

Zedner, L. 2005. Securing liberty in the face of terror: Reflections from criminal justice. *Journal of Law and Society* 32 (4): 507–533.

CHAPTER TWO

THE INTERNATIONAL REGULATION OF TRANSNATIONAL CRIMINAL LAW

DONALD FEAVER

Abstract

The attacks of 11 September 2001 were the catalyst for a re-examination of the conceptualisation and classification of several aspects of international law. Rather than being just a jargonistic term to denote some form of extra-national dimension, in much the same way the term "globalisation" has come to be used, the term "transnational law" has gradually taken on a specific legal meaning in recent years. Not only does transnational law have a technical significance but a growing number of scholars argue that transnational law is gradually emerging as a sub-branch of international law in its own right. This paper examines several questions related to the classification of international law. To answer the question whether "suppression crimes" are being correctly labelled as "transnational", we must first ask: what is transnational law? Is the term simply a convenient label denoting some form of legal globalisation, or does it have a legitimate jurisprudential foundation and function as an emerging sub-branch of international law? Assuming that it does have legitimate significance, a second question is: as a specific sub-branch of international criminal law having its own unique substantive character and administrative processes, does "transnational criminal law" qualify as a specialised system of law having the characteristics of a transnational regulatory regime?

1. Introduction

It is difficult to imagine how anything constructive could possibly emerge from the terrorist attacks of 11 September 2001. Nevertheless, the attacks became something of a catalyst leading to an examination of a number of issues surrounding the conceptualisation and classification of several aspects of international law. The need for this exercise was identified in late 2001 by Antonio Cassese who commented that in addition to the human and psychological impacts, the attacks had "shattering consequences for international law… subverting some important legal categories, thereby imposing the need to re-think them" (Cassese 2001). Cassese's comments were primarily directed towards the pressing need to clarify the status of terrorism as an international crime Cassese, 2006). However, the process of clarifying the status of terrorism indirectly raised a range of questions relating to the status of the sub-branch of international criminal law known as "suppression crimes" within the broader context of international law as a whole.

It is probable that Neil Boister neither realised nor intended to engage in either of these challenges when he published an important article in 2003 advocating the need to re-classify "suppression crimes" as a specific body of international criminal law to be known as "transnational criminal law". In that article, he states that "transnational crime can be constructed by recasting an existing sub-category of international criminal law as transnational criminal law". Although the term was then "unknown to international lawyers", Boister explains that his reason for choosing "transnational criminal law" was that the term "transnational crime" is "commonly used by criminologists, criminal justice officials and policymakers" (Boister 2003).

What he did not mention, however, is that his choice may also be particularly appropriate for a number of jurisprudential reasons in addition to its complementary associations with criminology. Rather than being just a jargonistic term to denote some form of extra-national dimension (Berman 2005; id. 2007), much in the same way the term "globalisation" has come to be used (Feaver 2009), the term "transnational law" has gradually taken on a specific legal meaning in recent years. Not only does transnational law have a technical significance but a growing number of scholars argue that transnational law is gradually emerging as a sub-branch of international law in its own right.[1]

The discourse surrounding the re-classification of that sub-branch of "suppression crimes" provides a unique opportunity to broaden the discussion. Accordingly, it is within the context of international criminal

[1] For a discussion of the meaning of "transnational" in the context of this article, see Cata Backer, Larry. 2007. Principles of transnational law: The foundations of an emerging field. *Law at the End of the Day*, 9 March 2007, http://lcbackerblog.blogspot.com.

law that this chapter examines two questions related to the classification of international law. To answer the question whether "suppression crimes" are being correctly labeled as "transnational", we must first determine what transnational law is. Is the term simply a convenient label denoting some form of legal globalisation, or does it have a legitimate jurisprudential foundation and function as an emerging sub-branch of international law? Assuming that it does have legitimate significance, a second question is: as a specific sub-branch of international criminal law having its own unique substantive character and administrative processes, does "transnational criminal law" qualify as a specialised system of law with the characteristics of a transnational regulatory regime? This question is relevant within the context of recent International Law Commission efforts to better understand the role and position of specialised bodies of law within the broader context of international law.

The chapter is structured as follows. In Section 2, the term "transnational law" is defined and examined using several competing analytical approaches for classifying international law. This is followed by an examination in Section 3 as to whether "suppression crimes" qualify as transnational within the context of these approaches. In Section 4, the question whether, or the extent to which, these suppression crimes qualify as a "transnational regulatory regime" is considered. A summary and conclusions are presented in the final section.

2. Background and Context: Conceptualising Transnational Law

Although the notion that transnational law could qualify as a sub-branch of international law is novel, the concept of "transnational" is not new to international law. The term is said to have been coined by Philip Jessup who first used it in a series of lectures and essays in 1956 (Jessup 1956). The subject of the lectures concerned certain developments occurring within the international legal order that were becoming more pronounced, especially in the aftermath World War II.[2] In his essays, Jessup describes the emergence of a species of law in respect of which:

---

[2] Although the term "transnational law" was also being used in a much narrower context by international legal scholars such as Percy Corbett and Arthur Nussbaum around the same time as the Storrs Lectures, Jessup was the first to develop and popularise a more comprehensive conceptualisation of international law including non-state actors. For example, see: Nussbaum, Arthur. 1954. *A concise history of the law of nations*, 2nd rev. edn, xi–xiii, 144–185, 291–306. New York: Macmillan; Corbett, Percy E. 1955. *The study of international law*, p. 50. Garden City, NY:

> I shall use, instead of "international law", the term "transnational law" to include all law which regulates actions or events that transcend national frontiers. Both public and private international law are included, as are other rules which do not wholly fit into such standard categories (Jessup 1956: 2).

Admittedly, the definition is sweeping. However, Jessup may have intended a slightly narrower meaning than that which appears upon first reading. As noted by Scott, this slightly narrower meaning is directed towards all "law" involved in regulation – what is called with increasing frequency, the "governance" – of the *transnational* ("actions or events that transcend national frontiers", whether involving state or non-state actors) (Scott 2009). Of particular significance is the inclusion of "non-state" actors in this definition, as is discussed in further detail below.

What led Jessup and another of his contemporaries, Wilfred Jenks, to ponder the issue was that both scholars had identified numerous examples of international norms that did "not wholly fit into [the] standard categories of public international or private international law". Public international law had, for the better part of a century, been conceptualised and defined by legal positivists as "the law of nations" (Kelson 1952; Lauterpacht 1958). That is to say, international law is a body of rules that regulates the relations between sovereign nation states (Shaw 2008). Because human beings and other sub-national entities such as non-governmental organisations and companies do not fall within the scope of this definition, they are not regarded as "subjects" of international law (Janus 1984).[3]

2.1 Subject-based Approach to Classifying International Law

The origin of this approach to classifying international law can be traced to the creator of the term, Jeremy Bentham, who in 1780 sought to categorise laws "on the basis of the persons whose conduct is the object of the law" (Janus 1984). Stated another way, Bentham was the originator of the "subject-based" approach to categorising law on the "basis of the subjects to be governed" (Bentham 1789). Since Bentham (erroneously, it will be argued below) concluded that international law only had sovereign

---

Doubleday;

Tietje, C., A. Brouder and K. Nowrot, eds. 2006. Philip C. Jessup's transnational law revisited: On the occasion of the 50th anniversary of its publication. *Essays in Transnational Economic Law* 50.

[3] This section draws heavily upon Janis, M. 1984. Individuals as subjects of international law. *Cornell International Law Journal* 17: 61.

nation states as its subjects, the subject of international law was "mutual transactions between sovereigns as such" (Bentham 1789). Although he did not create the term "private international law", a distinction left to Justice Story several decades later, Bentham did state that "as to any transactions which may take place between individuals who are subjects of different states, these are regulated by the internal laws, and decided upon by the internal tribunals" of individual sovereign states (Janus 1984: 364).

The definition of international private law was later "crafted" by Story to parallel Bentham's definition of public international law, thereby reinforcing "the notion that the individual was not a proper subject of international law". Widely credited as being the creator of modern conflict of laws with the publication of his treatise in 1834, Story sought to develop rules and methods to determine the appropriate choice of law and forum to apply in the event of a dispute between parties from different jurisdictions. According to legal positivists, because the subject of private international law is individuals, who are in turn the subjects that fall under the control of sovereign nations, private international law is "law" but not really "international". As a consequence, with few exceptions, the subject-based approach of positivist legal theories of international law are fashioned on the basis that "individuals are not proper subjects of public international law" (Jenks 1953).

Because the notion that "individuals are not proper subjects of public international law" had become so entrenched as orthodoxy by the mid-20th century, it was only natural that international lawyers such as Jessup and Jenks should identify and struggle with the definition's many anomalies. Rather than attempting to re-formulate the definition, it may have seemed to Jessup that creating a new, more expansive term may have been the easier alternative. Since then, however, the term "transnational law" has come to be more closely associated with the emergence of a new category or sub-branch of international law, seen as occupying that space between public international law on the one hand and private international law on the other.

2.2 Source-based Approach to Classifying International Law

An alternative approach to determining whether law is public international, private or transnational which is favoured by those investigating "transnationalism" is a source-based approach. This approach originated in a time preceding Bentham when Blackstone "distinguished his law of nations from other sorts of law not on the basis of its subjects but because of its sources". Therefore, the key distinguishing feature using a source-based approach is not whether it its subject is "states" or "non-states"; it is whether the source of the norms is "international, national or private" in origin. In applying such an approach, Blackstone recognised that the affairs of commerce were regulated by a law of their own called the "law merchant" (*lex mercatoria*) (Kasirer 1999):

> which all nations agree in and take notice of and it is particularly held to be part of the law of England which justifies the causes of merchants and the general rules which obtain in all commercial countries (Blackstone 1789).

In 1759, Lord Mansfield stated that "Mercantile law is not the law of a particular country but the law of all nations".[4] In any case, *lex mercatoria* is often cited as a non-state law system that falls into that class of international norms that Jessup identifies as "rules which do not wholly fit into such standard categories" (Jessup 1956: 2).

Since the end of World War II, as Jessop and Jenks identified, much diversity in the sources and types of international norm have emerged. More importantly, these norm-creation mechanisms blur the previously clear public law/private law divide. In acknowledging that the "global arena is populated by a multitude of norm makers and rule producers" (Zambansen 2006) both public and private, involved in the creation of both "hard and soft" norms, the subjects and sources of international law are now more complex than ever (Abbott and Snidal 2000). The acceleration and deepening of the globalisation process has resulted in the intensification of cross-border activity. Globalisation has resulted in increasing capital and information flows and human mobility (including criminal activity) as well as the mounting number of global issues such as the spread of disease, diminishing bio-diversity and human-induced climate change. The demand for international norm creation is out-pacing the supply ability of traditional methods of international public law creation. As a result, there has been an increase in non-state norm creation activity in a broad range of areas including corporate social responsibility initiatives, international commercial standard creation and the governance of technologies such as the internet.

2.3 A Hybrid Approach

The positivist approach, which regards the individual as not being a proper subject of international law, applies this principle at a systemic level. It is a principle that nation states, acting as gatekeepers, use to

[4] *Luke* v. *Clyde* [1759] 2 Burr 882 p. 887.

control individuals' access to international courts and tribunals. As Higgins notes, "states are such influential participants in the international system, they have until now been able to block the access of individuals to certain arenas, including notably the International Court" (Higgins 1994). However, she goes on to state:

> It has been suggested by one learned author [Carl Aage Norgaard] that the weakness of the positivist view on the place of individuals is that it fails to distinguish between the possession of rights and duties and the procedural capacity to sue or be sued on them. Norgaard contends that co-terminosity is not a prerequisite to acknowledgement as a subject of international law. He points to the dictum of the permanent Court of International Justice in 1932 that "it is scarcely necessary to point out that the capacity to possess civil rights does not necessarily imply the capacity to exercise those rights oneself".

The argument that there is no bar to individuals being the subject of rights and duties under international law paves the way for a further approach to be posited (Tucker 1965). This alternative "hybrid" approach conceives of "international law" as combining elements of both the traditional "subject-based" and the "source-based" approaches. The hybrid approach requires that the positivist state-centric view of international law be set aside in favour of a competing vision of international law and the legal system. As such, if the international legal system is regarded as a normative system comprised of numerous different sources of norms, both public and private, which accepts individuals as the normative subject of law, a different conceptualisation of international law emerges.

In order for this different conceptualisation to emerge, it must first be recognised that the positivist principle that only states are the subject of international law is a systemic-level assumption. Accordingly, if the focus of analysis is shifted from the level of system to the level of the norm, irrespective of whether is it "hard or soft, public or private", there are countless examples in international law where individuals are regulated by means of norms that specifically identify the individual as both the "subject and object" of the regulation (Manner 1952). The presence of this positivist systemic constraint does not diminish the reality that norms derived from public international law sources (as with non-state law sources) do directly regulate individuals as both the "subject and object" of the norm. For example, Article 2 of the *Optional Protocol to the ICCPR* provides that "individuals who claim that any of their rights enumerated in the Covenant have been violated and who have exhausted all available domestic remedies may submit a written communication to the Committee for consideration".[5]

If viewed as a normative system, the international system is capable of producing: (1) norms derived from a range of different sources including public and private non-state law systems and (2) different types of norms, i.e., hard and soft, which have (3) different subjects i.e., states and individuals and (4) different objects, e.g., states, individuals, space, oceans, plants and animals can all be the objects of regulation. A matrix of the range of different permutations and combinations of norms is provided in Table 1 below.

Table 1

Source	Subject	Object	Type	Classification
International Public	State	State	Hard/soft	Public International Law
	State	Individual	Hard/soft	Public International Law
	Individual	Individual	Hard/soft	Transnational Law
International Non-State	Individual	Individual	Soft	Transnational Law
National	State	State	Hard	Public International Law
	Individual	Individual	Hard	Private International Law

Of particular significance for the purposes of this chapter is the possibility of classifying international law derived from a public international source and with individuals as the subject and object of a norm (which may have the status of being hard or soft law) as transnational law. The justification for classifying it as such can be traced to Jessup's original definition in which he refers to "public and private international law... [and] other rules which do not wholly fit into such standard categories... whether involving state or non-state actors" (Jessup 1956). This justification for the classification resolves a range of potential conflicts that arise in classifying a diverse range of norms such as the Unidroit General Principles (transnational soft law) or a hybrid regulatory regime such as the public/private inter-relationship between the International Civil

[5] Article 2, Optional protocol to the ICCPR, G.A. res. 2200A (XXI), 21 U.N. GAOR Supp. (No. 16) at 59, U.N. Doc. A/6316 (1966), 999 U.N.T.S. 302 (entered into force 23 March 1976).

Aviation Organization (ICAO)(public international hard law) and the International Air Transport Association (IATA)(a private non-state law system).

3. Defining "Suppression Crimes" as Transnational Law

As mentioned in the introduction, in his 2003 article, Neil Boister suggested that a specific body of international criminal law be re-classified as "transnational criminal law" (Boister 2003). The justification for choosing "transnational", Boister noted, was that the term was already widely in use among criminologists and practitioners. However, the question considered in this section is whether this body of international norms might qualify as transnational for strong jurisprudential reasons as well. Accordingly, the purpose of this section is to reconsider Boister's choice of the term "transnational criminal law" by examining the sources and substantive normative characteristics of this sub-branch of international criminal law in light of the preceding discussion.

International crime has long occupied a specific place within the broader landscape of international law. The traditional notion of international crime includes a collection of offences that originate from customary norms[6] that address criminal acts that "shock the conscience of humanity" and involve some form of violation of human rights (Nagle 2010). Although human beings are both perpetrators and victims of these crimes (hence being both the subject and object of norms prohibiting such actions), this body of international criminal law has long been considered as "public international law". Avoidance of the issue of non-state actor involvement has occurred in two ways. First, these offences require that the crime be committed by a state or by a non-state actor *acting in a public or official capacity* (i.e., a representative of a state)[7] Second, rather than focusing on any injury to the victims of these crimes, international law has tended to treat the injury as one to the international community (Nagle 2010). Hence, the crime is an official act of state or that of an official of a state acting in a public capacity.

The body of international criminal law that is the subject of this examination falls into a different category of international crimes. While

---

[6] Now codified under the Treaty of Rome, the International Criminal Court has universal jurisdiction to prosecute these crimes (i.e., to prosecute offences to which international criminal liability attaches) on the basis that these offences constitute a "crime against humanity".

[7] A contrasting view is put forward by Marks and Clapham that state-actor involvement is not a necessary pre-condition.

most of the attention surrounding the international law concerning crime has been directed towards traditional offences such as war crimes, aggression, crimes against humanity, genocide and torture,[8] a very different category of international criminal law covering areas of activity such as terrorism, trafficking of drugs, people and arms, and money laundering, has been developing in the background since the early 1960s. One of the reasons that this more obscure category of international law has not attracted the attention of international public law scholars is that it defies many of the traditional conceptualisations and classifications of the international legal order.

Transnational criminal offences, by contrast, are offences that are neither committed by public officials nor crimes that "injure the international community". Boister defines the "suppression conventions" that form the main source of transnational criminal law as:

> crime control treaties concluded with the purpose of suppressing harmful behaviour by non-state actors ranging from counterfeiting to corruption, drug prohibition to the financing of terrorism, can already, it is submitted, be said to establish a system of [transnational criminal law]. These conventions provide, through a range of complex provisions for the criminalization by state parties in their domestic law of certain offences, for severe penalties, for extra-territorial jurisdiction, and for a variety of procedural measures (Boister 2003).

The transnational element in a non-legalistic sense is that the crime is committed in more than one state or the effect is felt in another state. This is particularly relevant in the case of terrorism where terrorist groups, for example, establish cells that operate across borders and the financial and human resources used to commission the act of terrorism are derived from a number of places (DFAT 2004). The indirect suppression of a transnational crime by international law can only ever be indirect because international law has no jurisdiction to enforce the rules against private individuals who are non-state actors. This is because the theory posits that international law cannot impose obligations or give rights directly to

---

[8] An international crime derived from customary international law can be defined as "an act universally recognized as criminal, which is considered a grave matter of international concern and for some valid reason cannot be left within the exclusive jurisdiction of the state that would have control over it under ordinary circumstances". *US v. List et al.*, 19 February 1948, Trials of War Criminals before the Nuernberg Tribunals under Control Council Law No. 10. Washington, DC: US Government Printing Office, 1950 Vol IX: 1230, 1241.

individuals because the individual is not a subject but an object of international law (Jessup 1956).

The subject and type of norms derived from two different sources associated with this sub-branch of international criminal law are considered below.

3.1 International Legislation: Security Council Resolution 1373

An extraordinary form of international law emerged as a consequence of the September 11 attacks. This form of law has since become widely referred to as "international legislation".[9] Although the term "international legislation" has been widely used in the past to refer to all manner of international law creating activity, the nature of the obligations created by the United Nation's Security Council through its adoption of Resolution 1373 is unique in several respects. These obligations have several dimensions with transnational implications which are discussed below.

Resolution 1373 was adopted unanimously by the Council on 28 September 2001. In it, the Council proscribed a range of measures <u>all</u> states would be required to pursue to combat terrorism. In Resolution 1373 the Security Council stated that all states would be required to undertake several actions to prevent the financing of terrorist attacks. Those actions, *inter alia*, required all states to prevent and suppress the financing of terrorism through the criminalisation of the collection of funds for terrorism purposes, to freeze the funds and assets of terrorists and persons associated with terrorism and to prohibit nationals from obtaining funds or resources to be used for terrorism directly or indirectly.[10] The Angolan representative stated in the Council debate on 22 April 2004 that "by adopting resolution 1373 (2001), the Security Council took the unprecedented step of bringing into force legislation binding on all States on the issue of combating terrorism" (Talmon 2005). These comments highlight the first distinguishing characteristic of Resolution 1373 in that it created "legislation binding on all States" (Schrivjer 2004). Stated another way, Resolution 1373 was the first resolution adopted that imposed obligations of a *general and abstract character*.

As an instrument of a general and abstract character, the question arises whether such legislation can only be made through negotiation

---

[9] The term "international legislation"has been widely used in the past to mean a range of different types of law-making activity including international law making by treaty and customary law. However, it must be noted that the term has always been used loosely.

[10] UN Security Council Resolution 1373 (2001) of 28 September 2001.

among nation states in the form of an international agreement. In the sense that Resolution 1373 is general and abstract, as Talmon notes, "these may well be triggered by a particular situation, conflict, or event, but they are not restricted to it. Rather, the obligations are phrased in neutral language, apply to an indefinite number of cases, and are not usually limited in time" (Talmon 2005). The basic characteristic of this new type of legislative or generic resolution is, as the Colombian delegate to the Security Council stated, that it "does not name a single country, society or group of people" (Talmon 2005). It can, therefore, be distinguished from the more conventional form of Security Council resolution targeted to a specific set of circumstances. It should be noted, however, that the Security Council has been criticised for its opportunistic approach to Resolution 1373 in that it has been argued that the Security Council acted outside its scope and if challenged before the International Court, it may well be found to be an *ultra vires* act (Rosand 2003).

The second aspect of Resolution 1373 has a more direct bearing on the issue of transnational law. In reference to the different types or forms of transnational law mentioned in Section 2.1, Resolution 1373 contains several examples of international law that make private individuals or entities both the subject and the object of international obligations. For example, Paragraph 2 states that "all States shall… [f]reeze without delay funds and other financial assets or economic resources of persons who commit, or attempt to commit, terrorist acts or participate in or facilitate the commission of terrorist acts". The question that arises is whether, within the context of the matrix of international law norms set out in Section 2.2, Resolution 1373 qualifies for being classified as transnational law.

As noted in the matrix, to qualify, the norm in question must be derived from an international source and both the subject and the object of the norm must be directed towards regulating individuals. In the case of Resolution 1373, it is clear that the object of the norm is "individuals" being "persons who commit, or attempt to commit, terrorist acts". It is also equally clear that the obligation being imposed, being the "freezing without delay funds and other financial assets or economic resources", is one that is imposed on states. Therefore, Resolution 1373 can be characterised as international public law in that it is primarily directed towards regulating state action.

3.2 International Treaty Obligations

In addition to Resolution 1373, the broad range of criminal acts that fall within the scope of transnational criminal law are known as "treaty crimes" (UN 2010). The earlier conventions create offences for issues such as hijacking of aircraft,[11] civil aviation matters[12] and hostage taking.[13] The later conventions deal with the issues of direct attacks using bombing and nuclear materials and also the financing of terrorism.[14] In addition to being distinguishable from traditional international crimes in that they are not derived from customary international law (mentioned in Section 2.2), treaty crimes also differ in that they do not give rise to international criminal responsibility. Instead, treaty crimes are a specific type of international obligation that, rather than giving rise to international jurisdiction under international law, merely subject nation states to proscribe certain types of acts as criminal offences under national law as well as to cooperate with other states in respect of their investigation and punishment. As such, from this "it does not necessarily follow that such crimes entail international criminal liability". Hence, when viewed broadly, it suggests that the primary subject and object of these obligations is the nation state rather than non-state actors.

In shifting the focus from a systemic to a normative level of analysis, all of the conventions directly criminalise the actions of a person involved with the offence. For example, the first suppression treaty, the 1963 Convention on Offences and Certain Other Acts Committed on Board Aircraft (the Tokyo Convention) discusses the restraint of a person who may be reasonably believed to be about to or to have committed an

---

[11] Convention on Offences and Certain Other Acts Committed on Board Aircraft 1963 (Tokyo Convention), opened for signature 14 September 1963, 704 UNTS 219 art 3 (entered into force 4 December 1969); Convention for the Suppression of Unlawful Seizure of Aircraft 1970 (The Hague Convention), opened for signature 16 December 1970, 860 UNTS 105 art 1 (a) (b) (entered into force 14 October 1971).

[12] Convention for the Suppression of Unlawful Acts against the Safety of Civil Aviation, opened for signature 23 September 1971, 974 UNTS 177 (entered into force 23 January 1973).

[13] Hostages Convention, opened for signature 17 December 1979, 1316 UNTS 205 (entered into force 3 June 1983).

[14] Terrorist Bombings Convention, opened for signature 15 December 1997, 2149 UNTS 284 (entered into force 8 February 1987); Terrorism Financing Convention, opened for signature 9 December 1999, 2178. UNTS 229 (entered into force 10 April 2002); Convention for the Suppression of Acts of Nuclear Terrorism, opened for signature 13 April 2005, 2245 UNTS 89 (entered into force 7 July 2007).

offence by the aircraft commander until disembarking from the aircraft where the person can be delivered to the authorities to be prosecuted under the appropriate state's law.[15] The 1970 Convention for Suppression of Unlawful Seizure of an Aircraft makes it an offence for a person to unlawfully seize control or attempt to unlawfully seize control of an aircraft.[16]

An example of a norm having the characteristics illustrative of many falling within this sub-branch of criminal law is found in Article 2 of the International Convention for the Suppression of Acts of Nuclear Terrorism. Article 2:1 provides that: "Any person commits an offence within the meaning of this Convention if that person unlawfully and intentionally:

(*a*) Possesses radioactive material or makes or possesses a device:

(i) with the intent to cause death or serious bodily injury; or

(ii) with the intent to cause substantial damage to property or to the environment".[17]

An analysis of the source, subject and object of this provision indicates that even though it is derived from a public international law source, both the subject and the object of the provision clearly are "individuals". Therefore, this class of international norm falls outside the scope of the traditional definition of what constitutes public international law. Accordingly, it can be argued that the normative character of much of this body of law would qualify as "transnational law", thereby reinforcing Boister's choice of the term.

4. The International Regulation of Transnational Crime

The second question considered in this chapter is whether, or to what extent, the regulation of transnational criminal law also qualifies as forming a transnational regulatory regime. The basis for and relevance of this question stem from a recent International Law Commission enquiry into the "fragmented" appearance of international law owing to a

---

[15] Convention on Offences and Certain Other Acts Committed on Board Aircraft 1963 (Tokyo Convention), opened for signature 14 September 1963, 704 UNTS 219 art 3 (entered into force 4 December 1969).

[16] Convention for the Suppression of Unlawful Seizure of Aircraft 1970 (The Hague Convention), opened for signature 16 December 1970, 860 UNTS 105 art 1 (a) (b) (entered into force 14 October 1971).

[17] UN General Assembly, International Convention for the Suppression of Acts of Nuclear Terrorism, opened for signature 13 April 2005, A/59/766.

proliferation of self-contained or specialised law systems that have come to cover the international legal landscape (Koskenniemi 2006).

The term "regulation" has many different meanings. In an abstract sense, a regulation is a rule or norm that is designed to influence a change in an actor's behaviour. More technically, a regulation is often defined as a form of subordinate legislation. However, more recently, regulation has become synonymous with a phenomenon known as the delegation of governance powers to specialised institutional bodies, both within and beyond the nation state, that administer specialised bodies of rules. In this chapter, the term "regulation" is used to describe a discrete "system of law" (Feaver 2006). Several criteria define what constitutes a specialised law system with regulatory characteristics. These criteria include:

- a specific or specialised body of substantive and procedural rules;
- an organisational framework and construct that is given the responsibility and delegated governance powers to administer those rules;
- some form of in-built mechanism to compel compliance with the rules;
- provision for enforcement and penalty in the case of non-compliance.

Given that the first criterion is satisfied in light of the discussion in Section 3, it is clear that transnational criminal law is comprised of an identifiable body of norms that fall within a specific subject matter area, namely, crimes that have a transnational dimension causing them to be "crimes of international concern". Although the 13 treaties and three protocols that comprise this body of norms cover different types of crimes, all 16 bodies of norms conform to the same general formula in terms of the character and composition of the norms.

The second criterion referred to above requires that the specialised body of law be overseen and administered by an organisational construct (i.e., an identifiable regulatory or administrative body) that is responsible for the administration of the rules. In this context, three United Nations bodies are the focus of this discussion. The first administrative body that is responsible for the oversight and administration of transnational criminal law is also a product of Security Council Resolution 1373. Resolution 1373 created a body called the Counter Terrorism Committee (CTC) to monitor the implementation of the obligations contained in Resolution 1373. The CTC works closely with another UN agency, the Counter Terrorism Executive Directorate (CTED), to implement the policies of the CTC and to assess member states' terrorism legislation and assists member states with technical assistance in support of legislative reform and other counter-terrorism initiatives. The CTC also works alongside the UN Office of Drugs and Crime (UNODC) Terrorism Prevention Branch (TPB) to ensure compliance. The UNODC TPB also provides support for CTC and CTED policy and facilitation programs which provide technical assistance to member states.[18]

Whether a body is a regulatory or administrative body is determined on the basis of the nature of the governance powers delegated to the body. Delegated governance powers can be one or a combination of: (1) rule-making powers, (2) executive/administrative/enforcement powers, and/or (3) adjudicative powers. The source of these governance powers is either a conferral of powers by nation states (usually in the form of an international treaty or agreement that constitutes the body [a constituent treaty]) or in the case of UN agencies, powers derived from a sub-delegation (Saaroshi 2007). A sub-delegation of powers arises where a superior body is empowered to create sub-bodies under its own constituent agreement. It can then confer powers that it is able to lawfully exercise under its constituent agreement to a properly constituted sub-body. It cannot, however, delegate governance powers that it does not possess. In the case of the UN bodies responsible for the administration of transnational criminal law, none of these bodies is vested with either rule-making or adjudicative powers. To the extent that these bodies are delegated executive/administrative powers, the scope and depth of those powers can be described as weak. The CTC has a weak policy-making power and the UN ODC and its TPB possess only basic administrative powers in the form of oversight and monitoring functions.

In regard to the third criterion, none of the treaties or protocols contains compliance mechanisms or enforcement provisions that are internal to the treaties. The extent to which an international regulatory regime is "self-contained" was examined by the International Court of Justice in the Tehran Hostages case. In Tehran Hostages, the Court identified how the Vienna Convention on Diplomatic Relations comprised a special and self-contained system of rules, distinct from the customary

---

[18] UNODC. 2010. *Working closely with the Security Council's CTC and CTED* www.unodc.org/unodc/en/terrorism/working-closely-with-ctc-of-the-security-council-and-cted.html?ref=menuside (accessed 11 October 2010);
UNODC. 2010. *UNODC's role in terrorism prevention* www.unodc.org/unodc/en/terrorism/the-role-of-unodc-in-terrorism-prevention.html?ref=menuside (accessed 16 October 2010).
"Technical assistance" is defined as the role of the UNODC TPB's branch experience at the operational level in dealing with other transnational crimes which lends itself to expert assistance in dealing with counter terrorism. As the TPB works with member states, it is able to report to the CTC any deficiencies in the counter terrorism programs.

international law of state responsibility.[19] In the event of any violations of the Vienna Convention, the ICJ determined that treaty signatories could not resort to remedies afforded by general international law. This was because the rules contained in the Vienna Convention "constitute a self-contained regime which... specifies the means at the disposal of the receiving State to counter any such abuse".[20] Although the Court, for the first time, mentioned the words "self-contained *regime*", it made a much more important structural observation. It recognised that the Vienna Convention contained its own "internal" mechanism for addressing and remedying breaches of the convention (Koskenniemi 2006).

In this regard, the regime established to oversee and administer transnational criminal law does not contain any special "internal" mechanisms for addressing and remedying breaches of the conventions. That is not to say, however, that general principles of international law are not applicable as conventional means of compelling compliance and providing remedies in the event of breach. Because the individuals who commit terrorist-related offences are not brought to account by the body that administers the rules, then it does not satisfy the final element required to be considered a fully developed transnational regulatory regime.

5. Conclusions

The questions this chapter has investigated relate to the classification of international law. Specifically, it seeks to answer the question whether "suppression crimes" are being correctly labeled as "transnational" by some international lawyers as well as criminologists and international law enforcement officials. In seeking to answer this question, we must first ask: what is transnational law? Is the term simply a convenient label denoting some form of legal globalisation, or does it have a legitimate jurisprudential foundation and function as an emerging sub-branch of international law? Assuming that it does have legitimate significance, a second question is: as a specific sub-branch of international criminal law with its own unique substantive character and administrative processes, does "transnational criminal law" qualify as a specialised system of law with the characteristics of a transnational regulatory regime?

The outcome of these investigations is that traditional approaches to classifying international law are now clearly redundant. The manner in

[19] Vienna Convention on Diplomatic Relations, opened for signature 24 April 1964, 500 UNTS 95 (entered into force 23 June 1961).

[20] Tehran hostages case, ibid, p. 48.

which the international legal space has evolved since World War II with the expansion in different sources, subjects and types of norms has meant that Philip Jessup's observation that new methods of international law classification are required is entirely justified. In a sense, Antonio Cassese's observation in 2001 that classifications relating to international criminal law require re-thinking is merely an extension of Jessup's earlier observations.

In focusing specifically upon crimes of international concern as a specialised sub-branch of international criminal law, it is found that Neil Boister's assertion that it should be re-classified as "transnational criminal law" is entirely justified for sound jurisprudential reasons. The norms that comprise transnational criminal law exhibit characteristics in terms of their subject and object that indicate that they fall within that category of international law which Jessup classified transnational. A further finding of this chapter is that while transnational criminal law does form a specialised body of law that is administered by dedicated organisational constructs, it does not yet satisfy the requirements to be classified as a fully developed transnational regulatory regime. The reason for this is that the regime lacks credible "internal" compliance and enforcement mechanisms.

References

Abbott, K.W. and D. Snidal. 2000. Hard and soft law in international governance. *International Organization* 54: 421–456.

Bentham, J. 1879. An introduction to the principles of morals and legislation. Oxford: Clarendon Press.

Berman, P. 2005. From international law to law and globalization. *Columbia Journal of Transnational Law* 43: 485.

—. 2007. Global legal pluralism. *Southern California Law Review* 80:1155.

Boister, N. 2003. Transnational criminal law? *European Journal of International Law* 14: 953, 954.

Cassesse, A. 2001. Terrorism is also disrupting some crucial legal categories of international law. *European Journal of International Law* 12 (5): 993–1001.

—. 2006. The multifaceted criminal notion of terrorism in international law. *Journal of International Criminal Justice* 4: 933.

Department of Foreign Affairs and Trade. 2004. *Transnational terrorism: Paper 2004*. Canberra: DFAT.

Feaver, D. 2006. The coherence of multilateral regulation. *Australian International Law Journal* 13: 33.

—. 2009. Globalization and national policy formation. *Critical Perspectives on International Business* 5 (3): 229.

Higgins, R. 1994. *Problems and process: International law and how we use it*. UK: Clarendon Press.

Janis, M. 1984. Individuals as subjects of international law. *Cornell International Law Journal* 17: 61.

Jenks, C. W. 1953. The conflict of law-making treaties. *British Year Book of International Law* 30: 401.

Jessup, P. 1956. *Transnational law,* p. 2. New Haven: Yale University Press.

Kelson, H. 1952. *Principles of international law*. Clark, NJ: The Lawbook Exchange.

Kasirer, N. 1999. Lexicographie mercatoria. *The American Journal of Comparative Law* 47 (4): 653–676.

Koskenniemi, M. 2006. *Fragmentation of international law: Difficulties arising from the diversification and expansion of international law*: Report of the Study Group of the International Law Commission, 58th session, Geneva, 1 May–9 June and 3 July–11 August 2006, p. 9. Geneva: International Law Commission.

Lauterpacht, E. 1958. *The development of international law by the International Court*. Cambridge: Cambridge University Press.

Manner, G. 1952. The object theory of the individual in international law. *The American Journal of International Law* 46 (3): 428–449.

Nagle, L. 2011. Terrorism and universal jurisdiction: Opening a Pandora's box? *Georgia State University Law Review* 5: 339.

Tucker, E. 1965. Has the individual become the subject of international law? *University of Cincinnati Law Review* 34: 341.

Rosand, E. 2003. Security Council Resolution 1373: The Counter-terrorism Committee, and the fight against terrorism. *The American Journal of International Law* 97 (2): 333.

Sarooshi, D. 2007. *International organizations and their exercise of sovereign powers*. Oxford: Oxford University Press.

Shaw, M. 2008. *International law*. Cambridge: Cambridge University Press.

Scott, C. 2009. "Transnational law" as proto-concept: Three conceptions. *German Law Journal* 10 (7): 879.

Schrivjer, N. 2004. September 11 and the challenges to international law. In *Terrorism and the UN*, eds Jane Boulden and Thomas G. Weiss. Indiana: Indiana University Press.

Talmon, S. 2005. The Security Council as world legislature. *American Journal of International Law* 99 (1): 175–193.
United Nations. 2010. *UN action to counter terrorism*, www.un.org/terrorism/ (accessed 13 October 2010).
Zumbansen, P. 2006. Transnational law. In *Encyclopaedia of comparative law*, ed. Jan Smits, 738–754. Cheltenham, UK; Northampton, MA: Edward Elgar.

CHAPTER THREE

AUSTRALIA'S RESPONSE TO THE WAR ON TERROR: A PREVENTATIVE AND DISPROPORTIONATE APPROACH AT THE COST OF HUMAN RIGHTS PROTECTIONS

ALPERHAN BABACAN

Introduction

The terrorist attacks on the New York Twin Towers on September 11, 2001, led to the passage of United Nations Resolution 1373 which placed a binding obligation upon all member states to take appropriate measures to restore international security and to suppress terrorism and terrorist groups. Since September 11, the risk of a terrorist attack has been portrayed as being an "exceptional" and "new threat" with indeterminate enemies. Western nations have stated that the unique nature of the threat justifies the implementation of exceptional preventative measures by governments to counter the "new threat". In many developed nations, such a view has led to the adoption of a "preventative" approach to terrorism through the introduction of new counter-terrorism laws (Zedner 2005). In Australia, counter-terrorism laws enacted since 2001 have created new criminal offences and provided extensive investigative, detention and questioning powers to police and intelligence agencies, which infringe upon traditional due process protections and civil liberties (Bronnitt and Stellios 2006).

As in the United States and the United Kingdom, the Australian Government's public justification for its legislative response to the "war on terrorism" is directed at preventing terrorism on the basis that, given the unique threat and the requisite urgency to act, the adoption of pre-emptive and preventative measures through war abroad and restrictive measures domestically are essential, as failure to act could have detrimental consequences should a threat of terrorism eventuate (Pickering, McCulloch and Neville-Wright 2007). The Howard Government argued that we were living in a more dangerous era and that it was essential for Australia to strengthen its counter-terrorism measures (Protecting Australia against Terrorism and Transnational Terrorism 2006; Transnational Terrorism: The Threat to Australia 2004). The Australian Security Intelligence Organisation (ASIO) has pointed out that given the "new threat", intervention by law enforcement and intelligence agencies may need to occur on the basis of partial or incomplete information and intelligence (ASIO 2005–2006).

In Australia, the adoption of a "preventative" approach to countering terrorism has resulted in the rapid enactment of new counter-terrorism laws, mainly at the Commonwealth level, since 2001. The legislation is directed at preventing terrorism by providing security agencies and the police with extensive search, detention and questioning powers (Lynch and Williams 2007; Syrota 2008). For example, the raft of counter-terrorism measures enacted in 2006 (including preventative detention, control orders and the increase of stop-and-question powers to police) after the London underground bombings was justified by the Australian Government on the basis that Australia's counter-terrorism laws were not adequate to prevent a London-style bombing and that the new measures would ensure that Australia would be in a better position to protect against a London-style terrorist attack (Ruddock 2006a, 2006b).

This chapter considers Australia's justifications for the war on terror and its suspension of human rights and due process protections with respect to terrorism-related offences. An overview of the literature relating to Australia's legislative response to terrorism reveals that the counter-terrorism measures implemented since 2001 have increased the powers of police and intelligence agencies, and reduced due process protections and judicial oversight (White 2004). The measures have adversely impacted upon due process protections and rights which have historically formed the cornerstone of Australia's criminal justice system. While Australia justifies its legislative response on the basis that the measures will "better protect" Australia and Australians from the threat of terrorism and terrorist attacks, the Australian Government has failed to publicly justify the exact nature and extent of the threat or how the measures will in actual fact reduce the risk of terrorism. While the need to protect Australia certainly is important, the legislative response shows a disregard for the human rights implications and an absence of the actuarial cost-benefit analysis which is normally associated with the enactment of legislation. It is argued that the counter-terrorism measures adopted in Australia are part of large-scale social control changes which are occurring in industrialised nations and are designed to control society. The chapter concludes by arguing that the suspension of due process protections are not justified because Australia has failed to adequately measure and justify both the threat of terrorism and how the implemented counter-terrorism measures will address the terrorist threat.

Australia's Legislative Regime and its Human Rights Implications

Prior to 2001, there was no terrorism-specific legislation in Australia (Lynch and Williams 2006). Political and religious violence in Australia was tried by various State and Commonwealth crimes acts under relevant sections relating to hijacking, damage to property, conspiracy, treason, and harm to life and property. The model was presumptive in nature in that all people charged of offences were deemed innocent until proven guilty and certain safeguards relating to detention, questioning, information and evidence gathering, and the privilege against self-incrimination were built into the criminal justice and investigative systems (Rose and Nesterovska 2007).

The legislative regime following the tragic events of September 11 changed many of these due process protections by providing increased police powers, reduced due process protections, increased executive powers and reduced judicial oversight (Syrota 2008). The immediate post-2001 measures which were implemented in 2002 focused on defining terrorism and terrorist acts and prescribing penalties. For example, the Security Legislation Amendment (Terrorism) Act 2002 amended the Criminal Code 1995 (Cwlth) at Schedule 1, Part 5.3, Division 100–103 and Part 2.4 to define terrorist acts and proscribed terrorist organisations (S. 102 Criminal Code 1995 [Cwlth]). The measures also gave ASIO increased investigative powers (Divisions 102, 104 and 105 of the Criminal Code and S. 80.2 Criminal Code).

The Australian Security Intelligence Organisation Legislation Amendment (Terrorism) Act 2003 increased ASIO's powers with respect to detaining and questioning terrorist suspects. Division 3, Part III, Section 34 enables ASIO to obtain questioning and/or detention warrants in order to obtain information about the planning and/or commission of terrorism offences. The warrants can be used to detain anyone who can substantially assist ASIO in collecting intelligence deemed to be important in relation to a terrorism offence (McCulloch and Tham 2005). Questioning warrants enable ASIO to detain a suspect for questioning without charge for renewable periods of seven days.

The Anti-Terrorism Act 2004 (Cwlth) introduced powers enabling the Australian Federal Police (AFP) to arrest a person for a terrorism-related offence and to detain them without charge for the purpose of investigating whether the person has committed a terrorism offence that an investigating official reasonably suspects the person has committed (Crimes Act 1914 [Cwlth], S. 23CA[1]). This period of detention can be extended for a further period by a magistrate (Crimes Act S. 23DA[7]). Built into the system is the concept of dead time (Crimes Act 1914 [Cwlth], S. 23CA[8]), whereby the time the suspect sleeps, eats a meal, contacts his/her lawyer and so forth is not counted as part of the detention period.

Following the terrorist attacks on the London underground in 2005, the Australian Government introduced a range of new powers, including Control Orders and Preventative Detention Orders; ministerial power to declare prescribed security zones; and police powers to stop, search and question persons in relation to terrorist acts (Anti-Terrorism Act [No. 2] 2005 [Cwlth]). The Act empowers courts exercising a federal jurisdiction to make Control Orders at the request of the AFP (Division 104 of the Criminal Code). Control Orders may be made by a court exercising a federal jurisdiction on the balance of probability that the making of the order would substantially assist in preventing a terrorist act and the obligations/prohibitions imposed on the person by the order are reasonably necessary to protect the public.

Under the National Security Information (Criminal and Civil Proceedings) Act 2004 (the NSIA), evidence in terrorism trials can be admitted in a closed hearing from which the defendant and/or his or her legal representative may be excluded. The Commonwealth Attorney General invokes this procedure by providing a certificate detailing why the Attorney General believes that the information disclosed or the presence of a person in court will prejudice national security. Following the closed hearing, the court must decide whether the information disclosed in the hearing can be released to the suspect or the suspect's legal representative. The legislation specifically directs the court that in making its decision, the court must provide the greatest weight to the certificate provided by the Attorney General.

As is demonstrably clear from the broad discussion above, Australia's legislative regime is premised upon the assumption that the pre-existing regime which provided due process protections and limited police powers was not adequate to counter the "new threat" of terrorism (Pickering and McCulloch 2010) and that a preventative and precautionary framework which is at odds with the protection of civil liberties and due process protections had to be adopted (see Zedner 2005).

There is an abundance of literature which critiques Australia's legislative regime in respect to its infringement of human rights and due process protections (Hocking 2004; UN Special Rapporteur 2006; McCulloch and Tham 2005; Pickering and McCulloch 2010; McCulloch 2002, 2003). The human rights impacts of the measures are aggravated by the fact that, unlike countries such as the United Kingdom, Canada and New Zealand, Australia is the only Western democratic country with no Bill or Charter of Rights to protect human rights (Williams 2003). In these other countries, counter-terrorism processes have been measured against their human rights charters and standards (Von Doussa 2006).

Control Orders and Preventative Detention Orders, for example, displace principles relating to extensive deprivation of liberty upon criminal conviction. Obligations which may be imposed by Control Orders (such as the wearing of a tracking device or confinement to a home) in order to "protect" the public from a terrorist act breach human rights principles relating to arbitrary detention (Article 9 [1] of the ICCPR) and the right of an individual to be informed at the time of arrest of the reasons for his or her arrest (Article 9 [2] of the ICCPR). These orders also breach the right of any person arrested or detained to be brought promptly before a judge to rule on the lawfulness of that detention (Article 9 [3] of the ICCCPR). Many of Australia's counter-terrorism laws and powers conferred in the various acts and the executive decision-making powers are excluded from review under Schedule 1 of the Administrative Decisions (Judicial Review) Act 1977 (ADJR) (Von Doussa 2006).

The counter-terrorism measures implemented in Australia are indeed exceptional in nature and depart from the traditional due processes offered by the criminal law. A central question posed by many academics, activists and lawyers is whether the exceptional measures are warranted. Has the suspension of due process protections been objectively measured and/or justified by the Australian Government? It is only by clearly answering this question that an objective assessment can be made as to whether the measures implemented are proportionate to the level of risk.

Are Australia's Measures Justified?

At the outset, as agreed by many scholars, it is acknowledged that the risk of terrorism is a real phenomenon (Willis 2008; Jore and Nja 2010; Carne 2008; Goldsmith 2008; O'Malley1992; Zedner 2005; Bronnitt 2004, 2010; Wilkinson 2010). However, the suspension of due process protections has been neither objectively and adequately measured nor justified by the Australian Government. On repeated occasions, the Australian Government has asserted that the counter-terrorism measures which give police and security personnel extensive powers have resulted in Australia being safer from a terrorist attack (Pickering and McCulloch 2010). Carne argues that the Australian Government has failed to articulate how Australia's counter-terrorism laws can eradicate and/or address the threat and that the government has relied upon imprecise references to the threat of terrorism (Carne 2008).

The classified nature of the information gathered by the police and the intelligence agencies prevents academic researchers from ascertaining how accurately organised crime and the risk of terrorist attacks are measured (Klerks 2007). However, there is ample literature on risk assessment which clearly documents the limitations associated with the manner in which risk is measured (Lupton 1999; Tierney 1999; Willis 2008; Aven and Kristensen 2005; Aradau and Van Munster 2007; Haines, Sutton and Phung 2008; Jore and Nja 2010; Willis 2008; Zedner 2005; Zoutendijk 2010). Determination of future risk is essentially a forecast of possibilities which may eventuate (Carmody 2010), as opposed to an actuarial calculation. Threats which may arise due to the suspension of due process protections become difficult to justify given that it is not possible to predict future risk with any certainty.

Writing from a regulatory perspective, Haines, Sutton and Phung (2008) emphasise that risk has three dimensions: *actuarial*, *social* and *political*. "Actuarial risk" assessment involves the quantification of the risk or the likely impact of risk of an adverse event (e.g., a terrorist attack) so as to enable legislators to put in place measures to reduce the probable harms of that risk. An actuarial assessment of risk focuses on an objective and rational calculation of risk so that appropriate regulatory measures are put in place. In many countries, including Australia, the threat of terrorism is measured at four levels (extreme, high, moderate and low) using qualitative, semi-quantitative and quantitative methodologies. The first two methodologies look at factors such as those influencing the probability of an attack and the effectiveness of the various counter-terrorism measures to combat the attack. The quantitative methodology involves numbers and probabilities of models of risk. All the methods involve matrices of various risks and the likelihood and possible consequences of an attack (Maguire 2000). Despite the incorporation of a range of factors, all the models provide mere estimations of the risk of a terrorist attack. The reliability of this data is further hampered by the fact that decisions about the gathering and interpretation of the intelligence available are made under urgent time pressure, often without accurate or full information being available to investigators. This can result in inconsistent and subjective interpretations and analysis of the data, which in turn can result in bias and inaccuracy (Kebbell, Muller and Martin 2010; Jarrett and Westcott 2010; Bammer 2010). Given this reality, mere estimations of the potential of a terrorist attack should not be used to enact legislation which suspends due process protections.

Further analysis of the literature on risk demonstrates that notions of risk and the legal responses required to respond to the perceived threat or risk are complex and are a product of human construction, which is socially, politically and culturally determined and constructed by governments, the police and the media (Lupton 1999; Tierney 1999; Willis 2008; Aven and Kristensen 2005; Aradau and Van Munster 2007). In discussing this concept, Haines, Sutton and Phung (2008) refer to the concept as *socio-cultural risk*. The authors also discuss *political risk*, which relates to the desire of governments to maintain credibility and legitimacy as they are charged with managing both actuarial and socio-cultural risk (Haines, Sutton and Phung 2008). Many societies fail to properly distinguish between these different types of risks. Distinguishing between these different concepts of risk is important as it is ultimately governments which put regulatory measures in place to combat or address a particular risk, and accuracy of the measurements is needed to determine the nature and extent of the measures that are put in place.

Haines, Sutton and Phung (2008) point out that following the September 11 terrorist attacks, the Australian Government relied upon socio-cultural and political notions of risk assessment as opposed to an actuarial assessment. The new counter-terrorism measures and their legislative framework created a sense that the Australian Government was doing something about terrorism and the risk of a terrorist attack (Haines, Sutton and Phung 2008). This has been confirmed by other writers in this field who argue that the calculation of the threat of terrorism has not been actuarial but has been speculative in nature, with little consensus among terrorism experts on whether the measures could identify and reduce terrorism (Carne 2008; Mythen and Walklate 2006, 2008). Haines, Sutton and Phung (2008) further stress that the legislative measures taken in Australia were not driven only by the need to protect but also to gain political legitimacy and to provide socio-cultural reassurance. The Government achieved this not only through the enactment of rafts of counter terrorism legislation but also through providing social assurance by means ofvarious risk narratives in the public domain (Haines, Sutton and Phung 2008).

Much of the focus of nation states in the 21st century revolves around gaining legitimacy (Wallerstein 2005). Glassner (2004) points out that three basic techniques are utilised to ramp up fear: repetition, use of narrative techniques and misdirection. By repeating the same message frequently, the message gains currency and validity. By constructing a narrative, e.g., the cultural construction of "risk", fear levels are increased. The construction of risk is a useful instrument for gaining political control and the conformity of citizens, helping to resolve the legitimacy crisis of the nation state. Writing specifically about Australia's counter-terrorism policies, Bronnitt (2004, 2010) points out that the Australian Government exploited the insecurity and fear created in the post September 11 climate to erode civil liberties and due process protections. Bronnitt (2010) maintains that while undertaken in the name of security and the need to protect Australia from terrorism, the enactments undertaken by the Australian Government were influenced by international pressure rather than an in-depth calculation of the actuarial risk of terrorism. This argument is reinforced by other authors such as Goldsmith (2008) and Carne (2008), who examined the manner in which the executive enacted the measures. Goldsmith (2008) states that the enactment of Australia's counter-terrorism measures was dominated by the executive and lacked proper parliamentary input.

In pushing for the enactment of Australia's counter-terrorism measures, the Government constantly emphasised the "unique threat" posed to Australia and the rest of the world by the terrorist attacks of and since September 11, with a general absence of any systematic review of the existing laws (Goldsmith 2008; Carne 2008). Legislation was enacted in a language and culture which placed emphasis on "urgency" (Carne 2008) to demonstrate that the Government was "doing all it could" to protect Australia from a terrorist attack (see Ruddock 2006 a, 2006b, 2007a, 2007b).

There was a lack of the public discussion and consultation which is normally associated with the enactment of major pieces of legislation. Very little time was allowed for parliamentary committees to scrutinise any submissions that had been received. Carne (2010, p. 50) highlights this point and states:

> Terrorism was legislated in haste with claims that adequate review and remedy would follow. This was used by the government to challenge legitimate alternative views and criticisms. There was a pattern of rapid legislative passage, few amendments, discounting and rejecting of parliamentary and other review committee recommendations and an unwillingness to remedy legislative deficiencies.

Much was borrowed from the United Kingdom in terms of definitions (for example of terrorism and terrorist-related activity) and concepts (such as control orders and preventative detention) (Bronnitt 2010).

Ericson and Haggerty (1997) argue that the counter-terrorism measures adopted in many countries are linked to the social changes occurring as a result of the fragmentation and insecurity caused by the process of globalisation. Fragmented communities respond to uncertainty through feelings of fear and insecurity. The management of insecurity is now a central function of governments and public and private institutions. Similarly, Goldsmith (2004) argues that the post September 11 counter-terrorism measures are part and parcel of a risk society which governments govern through this fear, enabling them not only to implement exceptional measures but in doing so to convince the populace that such measures (such as counter terrorism measures) are a small price to pay for their security. Imprecise and emotive references to terrorism are resorted to in order to justify preventative measures to address the so-called "worst case scenario" (Zedner 2005). Exploitation of this fear in turn enables governments to justify measures which erode civil liberties (Aradau and Van Munster 2007).

Conclusion

The erosion of civil liberties and due process protections is not justified in the absence of measurements and justification of the terrorism threat level and the actual impacts of counter-terrorism measures. Counter-terrorism laws which provide police and security personnel with increased investigative, detention and questioning powers contravene the historical protections afforded by the common law and the major international human rights treaties to which Australia is a signatory. The war on terrorism cannot be won by suspending human rights and due process protections. The way forward clearly lies in the better engagement of communities and the adoption of human rights frameworks with proper checks and balances designed to protect both human rights and the Australian public from terrorist attacks.

References

Arandau, C. and R. Van Munster. 2007. Governing terrorism through risk: Taking precautions, (un)knowing the future. *European Journal of International Relations* 13 (1): 89–115.

Australian Government Media Release. 2009. *Counter terrorism laws strengthened*. Media release, www.pm.gov.au/news/media_releases/media_Release1551.html (accessed 22 May 2009).

Australian Security Intelligence Organisation. 2006. *Report to Parliament 2005–2006.*

Aven, T. and V. Kristensen. 2005. Perspectives on risk: Review and discussion of the basis for establishing a unified and holistic approach. *Reliability Engineering and System Safety* 90 (1): 1–14.

Bammer, G., ed. 2010. *Dealing with uncertainties in policing serious crime*. Canberra: ANU E Press.

Bronitt, S. 2004. Australia's legal response to terrorism: Neither novel nor extraordinary. In *Human rights 2003: The year in review,* ed. T. Davis. Clayton: Monash University.

—. 2010. Preface. In *Dealing with uncertainties in policing serious crime*, ed. G. Bammer. Canberra: ANU E Press.

Bronitt, S. and J. Stellios. 2006. Sedition, security and human rights: Unbalanced law reform in the war on terror. *Melbourne University Law Review* 29: 923–960.

Carmody, T. 2010. Criminal law. In *Dealing with uncertainties in policing serious crime*, ed. G. Bammer, 101–113. Canberra: ANU E Press.

Carne, G. 2008. Hasten slowly: Urgency, discretion and review: A counter terrorism legislative agenda and legacy. *Deakin Law Review* 13 (2): 49–98.

Commonwealth of Australia. 2004. Protecting Australia against terrorism: Australia's national counter terrorism policy and arrangement. Canberra: Commonwealth of Australia.

Department of Foreign Affairs and Trade. 2004. *Transnational terrorism: The threat to Australia.* Canberra: Commonwealth of Australia.

Department of the Prime Minister and Cabinet (DPC). 2006. *Counter terrorism white paper: Securing Australia, protecting our community*. Canberra: Commonwealth of Australia.

Ericson, R. and K. K. Haggerty. 1997. *Policing the risk*. Oxford: Clarendon.

Glassner, B. 2004. Narrative techniques of fear mongering. *Social Research* 71 (4): 819–826.

Goldsmith, A. 2008. The governance of terror: Precautionary logic and counter-terrorist law reform after September 11. *Law and Policy* 30 (2): 142–167.

Haines, F., A. Sutton and C. Platania-Phung. 2008. It's all about risk, ain't it? Science, politics, public opinion and regulatory reform. *Flinders Journal of Law Reform* 10: 435–457.

Hocking, J. 2004. *Terror laws: The threat to democracy.* Sydney: New South Wales University Press.

Human Rights and Equal Opportunity Commission. 2008. *A human rights guide to Australia's counter terrorism laws.* Sydney: HREOC.

Jarrett, R. and M. Westcott. 2010. Quantitative risk. In *Dealing with uncertainties in policing serious crime,* ed. G. Bammer, 67–85. Canberra: ANU E Press.

Jore, C. H. and O. Nja. 2010. Risk of terrorism: A scientifically valid phenomenon or a wild guess? The impact of different approaches to risk assessment. *Critical Approaches to Discourse Analysis Across Disciplines* 4 (2): 197–216.

Kebbell, M. R., D. A. Muller and K. Martin. 2010. Understanding and managing bias. In *Dealing with uncertainties in policing serious crime*, ed. G. Bammer, 87–97. Canberra: ANU E Press.

Klerks, P. 2007. Methodological aspects of the Dutch national threat assessment. *Trends in Organised Crime* 10: 91–101.

Lupton, D. 1999. *Risk.* London: Routledge.

Lynch, A. and G. Williams. 2006. *What price security? Taking stock of Australia's anti-terror laws.* Sydney: UNSW Press.

Maguire, M. 2000. Policing by risks and targets: Some dimensions and implications of intelligence-led crime control. *Policing and Society* 9: 315–336.

McCulloch, J. 2002. War at home: National security arrangements post 11 September 2001. *Alternative Law Journal* 27 (22): 87–91.

—. 2003. Counter terrorism, human security and globalisation: From welfare state to warfare state. *Current Issues in Criminal Justice* 14: 283–298.

McCulloch, J. and J. Tham. 2005. Secret state, transparent subject: The Australian Security Intelligence Organisation in the age of terror. *The Australian and New Zealand Journal of Criminology* 38 (3): 400–415.

Mythen, G. and S. Walklate. 2006. Criminology and terrorism: Which thesis? Risk society or governability? *British Journal of Criminology* 46: 379–398.

Mythen, G. and S. Walklate. 2008. Terrorism, risk and international security: The perils of asking "what if?". *Security Dialogue* 39 (2–3): 221–242.

O'Malley, P. 1992. Risk, power and crime prevention. *Economy and Society* 21: 225–275.

Pickering, S. and J. McCulloch. 2010. The Haneef case and counter terrorism policing in Australia. *Policing and Society* 20 (1): 21–38.

Pickering, S., D. Wright-Neville, J. McCulloch and P. Lentini. 2007. *Counter-terrorism policing and culturally diverse communities.* Melbourne: Monash University.

Rose, G. and D. Nesterovska. 2007. Australian counter terrorism offences: Necessity and clarity in federal criminal law reforms. *Criminal Law Journal* 31 (20): 20–55.

Ruddock, P. 2006a. Strengthening counter-terrorism laws in Australia. *Jurist*, www.jurist.law.pitt.edu/forumy/2006/03/strengthening-counter-terrorism-laws.php (accessed 8 May 2010).

—. 2006b. A safe and secure Australia: An update on counter terrorism. *Original Law Review* 2 (40): 48–49.

—. 2007a. *Primary duty to protect our nation*. Press Release, 13 August 2007.

—. 2007b. Legislating against atrocities. *Lawyers Weekly* 16.

Syrota, G. 2008. Australia's counter terrorism offences: A critical study. *University of Western Australia Law Review* 34: 103–144.

Tierney, K. J. 1999. Towards a critical sociology of risk. *Sociological Forum* 14 (2): 215–242.

UN Special Rapporteur on the Promotion and Protection of Human Rights While Countering Terrorism. 2006. *Australia: Study on human rights compliance while countering terrorism*. UN Doc A/HRC/4/26/Add.3.

Van Doussa, J. 2006. Reconciling human rights and counter-terrorism: A crucial challenge. *James Cook University Law Review* 13: 104–123.

Wallerstein, I. 2005. After developmentalism and globalization, what? *Social Forces* 83 (3): 1263–1278.

White, J. 2004. *Defending the homeland: Domestic intelligence, law enforcement and security*. Thomson Wadsworth.

Wilkinson, S. 2010. The modern policing environment. In *Dealing with uncertainties in policing serious crime*, ed. G. Bammer, 15–26. Canberra: ANU E Press.

Williams, G. 2003. National security, terrorism and bills of rights. *Australian Journal of Human Rights* 8 (2): 263–273.

Willis, H. W. 2008. *Challenges of applying risk management to terrorism security policy: Testimony submitted for the record to the Committee on Homeland Security, Subcommittee on Transportation Security and Infrastructure Protection, United States House of Representatives, 24 June 2008*. California: Rand Corporation.

Zedner, L. 2005. Securing liberty in the face of terror: Reflections from criminal justice. *Journal of Law and Society* 32 (4): 507–533.

Zoutendijk, A. J. 2010. Organised crime threat assessments: A critical review. *Criminal Law and Social Change* 54: 63–86.

Commonwealth of Australia Legislation

Administrative Decisions (Judicial Review) Act 1977
Anti Terrorism Act 2004
Anti Terrorism Act (No. 2) 2004
Criminal Code 1995
Crimes Act 1914
National Security Information (Criminal and Civil Proceedings) Act 2004
Security Legislation Amendment (Terrorism) Act 2002
International Instruments
International Covenant on Civil and Political Rights: Resolution 1373, www.un.org/Docs/journal/asp/ws.asp?m=S/RES/1373(2001) (accessed 11 August 2010).

CHAPTER FOUR

THE RISING POLITICS OF "EMERGENCIES" IN THE GLOBAL AGE: A CRITICAL REFLECTION ON THE GOVERNANCE OF (IN)SECURITY IN AUSTRALIA

SELVER B. SAHIN

It is now almost an everyday practice to hear or read about how our increasingly inter-connected world is surrounded by so many "new" and "complex" forms and sources of "emergencies", such as intra-state violence, refugee flows, illegal immigration and terrorism, so it is argued that the world is becoming more and more dangerous than ever. Similarly, it is almost impossible to find a single policy document or strategy paper produced throughout the recent decades that does not refer to the "novelty" and "complexity" of contemporary "emergencies" or security "risks" conceptualised in relation to the changing nature of contemporary conflict associated with state capacity. Such documents often call for "joined up" or "whole-of-government" policies to improve administrative, institutional and functional state capacities with the purpose of better managing these "emergencies" or security risks threatening global (Western) peace and security.

This chapter attempts to critically examine the growing centrality of the concept of "emergencies" to the contemporary global politics of the governance of (in)security and its impact on the conception of security in Australia. Drawing upon Beck's analysis of "world risk society" and Agamben's formulation of Carl Schmitt's theory of "the state of exception" as a "dominant paradigm" for governance in the contemporary period, this chapter seeks to demonstrate the limits and contradictions of contemporary policies and practices of the governance of security challenges which are informed by a risk-management approach formulated within the framework of "whole-of-government" engagement. It argues that the contemporary politics of managing "emergencies" not only tends to perpetuate the dynamics of political intervention as a form of government through the construction of fear of the enemy but also provides a powerful discursive escape from responsibility for the policies and practices that are themselves more likely to create new "emergencies".

The chapter begins with a discussion of the conceptualisation of security as a political construct. The second part elaborates on conceptual and theoretical aspects of the growing relevance of "emergencies" to contemporary security policies on the basis of Beck's "world risk society" analysis and Agamben's critique of "exceptionalism" as a "paradigm of government". The third part discusses the implications of the increasing relevance of "emergencies" in the context of the conceptualisation of security in Australia. The final section presents concluding remarks.

Conceptualising Security

"Security" is a political construct that is conceptualised in the way it has been defined and addressed. It has traditionally been associated more with states and satisfying their interests than with people and their needs, and formulated on the basis of "national security" articulated within an interstate framework (Bilgin 2003). According to this way of conceptualising security, the security of states should come before that of individual people – that is, the protection of sovereignty and territorial boundaries of states is of paramount importance – and the undertaking of individual or collective militarisation is the most effective strategy for promoting a state's interests, defined in terms of power. These state-centric, external-military-threat-focused understandings of security, which formed the basis of the strategic studies and foreign policy agenda during the Cold War, were largely based on the perception that war for territorial and resource gains is always a possibility in inter-state relations, which can only be "controlled" by national leaders through military force and statecraft including diplomacy, deterrence and arms control (Walt 1991). This war-based thinking about security gave rise to arms races in an ideologically divided world and created new insecurities for societies, which became more apparent following the Chernobyl accident. Through the construction of fear of the enemy, this thinking also served to justify the pursuit of government policies restricting individual and collective rights and freedoms in both the developing and the developed parts of the world.

In the 1990s, in conjunction with the outbreak of intra-state violence in different parts of the world including Europe, which was driven by the disintegration of the Soviet Union and Tito's socialist Yugoslavia,[1] there was an intensification of academic works with alternative definitions of security, such as "cooperative security", "security cooperation", "comprehensive security", and "human security" that emphasised the individual, societal and global aspects of security (Nossal 1995; Bilgin 2003). There had been prior attempts to re-define the concept of security and its components, such as the concept of "common security" put forward in the early 1980s by the Palme Commission as an alternative conception of security to attract attention to the threat to the security of humankind posed by nuclear weapons (Nossal 1995; Bilgin 2003). However, in the 1990s the alternative definitions were more related to the growing willingness of policy-makers to re-think the meaning of security and embrace these academic efforts to "adorn" security (Nossal 1995; Hataley and Nossal 2004), especially the idea of human security, which prioritises the security of individuals and encompasses seven core, inter-related components of security to improve the quality of life, i.e., economic, food, health, environmental, personal, community and political (UNDP 1994).[2] As Nossal (1995) points out, a great deal of attention was given to the definitional aspects of alternative frameworks of security such as the broad conceptualisation of human security and its "all inclusive" or "open-ended" scope (see, for example, Paris 2001). The question of what has driven leading Western governments to embrace these alternative notions of security in the post-Cold-War era, on the other hand, has not attracted much scholarly interest (Nossal 1995). According to David Chandler (2008), however, human security is "the dog that didn't bark" in that its integration into the mainstream of Western policy making has not

---

[1] It should be noted that the Yugoslav wars triggered the biggest refugee influx to Western Europe since the Second World War. This is viewed by some analysts as one of the major factors that prompted the recognition of the Slovene and Croat declarations of independence. Preventing the refugee exodus also shaped the international engagement during the Bosnian war, reflected in the deployment of peacekeepers to facilitate the delivery of humanitarian relief to the so-called "safe havens", even though there was no peace to keep on the ground. For a critical discussion of the employment of international humanitarian assistance as an instrument of security policy to prevent large scale population movements, see Duffield 1997, 2001.

[2] The governments of Japan, Canada and Norway, for instance, adopted and incorporated human security into their foreign policy agenda to varying degrees, stressing its different aspects. They also formed a "human security network" with several other states and non-government organisations in 1999 and successfully campaigned for the universalisation of the ban on anti-personnel landmines and the establishment of the International Criminal Court.

produced real policy outcomes but has helped to reinforce, rather than challenge, existing hierarchies of power because human security approaches tend to exaggerate new post-Cold-War security threats, to locate these threats in the developing world and to facilitate short-term policy making in the absence of the geo-strategic Cold War order and the domestic framework of the politics of left and right.

The frequent policy references to the contradictory forces of globalisation and their effects on communities and societies – that is, progress, cooperation and integration on the one hand and disruption, exclusion, tribalism and fragmentation on the other hand – have come to dominate the current understanding of insecurity, conceptualised in relation to a complex and dangerous outside environment (see, for example, Boutros-Ghali 1992; Kaldor 1999). This current understanding is apparent in the emergence of a broad consensus on the changing nature of conflict in the post-Cold-War era that has come to be associated with "state failure" or "fragility" along the "troubled borderlands of the global order" (Duffield 2001). It is based on two main convictions. One is that today's conflicts, referred to as "new wars" (Kaldor 1999), which occur in the context of state disintegration or civil conflict, constitute the most serious threat to international stability because of their trans-boundary effects such as the spread of violence and instability to neighbouring countries and refugee flows (Boutros-Ghali 1992; Helman and Ratner 1992–3). The other basic conviction is that these wars, that it is argued are motivated by identity politics rather than legitimate political interests, are said to differ from past wars in terms of the use of organised violence against civilians and in the difficulty of ending them. This difficulty arises partly because those benefiting from the political economy of these wars (e.g., black market economies) strive to perpetuate the conditions of insecurity (Kaldor 1999; Bloomfield and Reilly 1998).

The September 11 attacks and the consequent global "war on terror" agenda have radically transformed contemporary perceptions of insecurity. This is reflected in recent works on "state failure" or "fragility" that are characterised by a tendency to measure the "stateness" of the world's states on the basis of a set of institutional and functional "benchmarks" derived from certain assumptions about "ideal" statehood (Milliken and Krause 2002). The degree to which states are perceived to be diverging from the "standard" and are argued to have "failed" determines their place on the "stateness" scale (see, for example, Foreign Policy's Failed State Index, World Bank's Governance Indicators). No matter how geo-strategically insignificant they are, states such as Somalia, Afghanistan, Sudan, Haiti and the Solomon Islands, where central government structures have little or no sovereign control beyond the capital and *fail* to deliver the security and development needs of their populations, are often cited as the source of global security threats that cannot be left to their own devices, especially in "a time of terror" (see, for example, Rotberg 2003; DFID 2005). The pursuit of governance-focused, "joined up" or "whole-of-government" policy responses, as is discussed further below, has in this context become central to the management of contemporary insecurities in an increasingly inter-connected world that has many uncertainties and risks (Beck 1999), ranging from pandemics and illegal immigration to drug trafficking and terrorism (Rotberg 2003; Fukuyama 2004).

A "World Risk Society" or a "Permanent State of Emergency": What Kind of World Are We Living in?

According to German sociologist Ulrich Beck, the concept of risk is not a matter of "mathematicised morality" of expert thinking that can easily be "reducible to the product of probability of occurrence multiplied with the intensity and scope of potential harm" (Beck 2006). Risk refers rather to a socially constructed phenomenon (ibid.) that can be defined as "a systematic way of dealing with hazards and insecurities induced and introduced by modernisation itself" (id. 1992: 21). Looked at this way, what we are facing today, Beck suggests, is a "world risk society" in which environmental, technological and financial risks and terrorism are, albeit unequally, distributed around the globe and processed through political means, manifested in the pluralisation of experts and public agencies involved in the definition, foresight and control of the future consequences of human action (id. 1999). There is, however, no way to protect from or insure against these contemporary dangers which recognise no spatial or technical boundaries and are likely to result in catastrophic, irreversible harm. Most of these risks, such as the crash of financial markets, technologic conflicts and ecological crises, Beck argues, are in effect human-made. They have been manufactured through the knowledge of the "controllability" of dangers by experts and industries worldwide. Specifically, they are the product of modern industrial society itself, deriving from institutional and social processes of capitalist modernisation and administrative and technical decision-making structures that seek to control uncertainties but fail to introduce social accountability and responsibility for the adverse socio-economic, ecological, technological and political effects these policy interventions and regulations create (ibid.).

Instead of clarifying responsibility and establishing accountability, the usual policy response has been to formulate new policy interventions or to re-invent old and proved to be ineffective solutions as new policy instruments to address these new problems and dangers, resulting in a kind of "organised irresponsibility" (id. 1999). After all, risk management is described as a strategic instrument that does not seek to create "perfect security" but to prevent a scenario from becoming real in today's complex and inter-dependent world facing new and "much less computable" dangers (Rasmussen 2006). Risk definition is, however, essentially a power game during the course of which some countries, sectors and corporations exercise a greater capacity to define risks for "others" in the global world of manufactured uncertainties (Beck 2006). The language of the complex and unpredictable nature of contemporary insecurities with possible catastrophic future effects in an increasingly inter-dependent world provides risk producers with a discursive immunity from individual and institutional responsibility and accountability.

An example of this approach is the "pre-emptive" military intervention in Iraq in 2003. The decision to wage war was justified as a necessary action to stop a "failed" or "rogue" state from providing weapons of mass destruction to terrorists, even though the UN nuclear watchdog International Atomic Energy Agency (IAEA) experts had found no evidence of weapons of mass destruction being possessed or developed by the Saddam Hussein regime. According to Michael Evans (2007), who strongly recommended Australia's adoption of an "integrated concept of security" informed by a risk management approach, the Iraqi war can only be understood in the context of "risk rationality" that focuses on consequences rather than on the capabilities and intentions of adversaries. This assessment appears to be more related to the future destructive effects of the use of weapons of mass destruction by terrorists than the probability of their possession or development by the Saddam Hussein regime. Regardless of the underlying political motives to justify the war on the basis of an imagined "worst case scenario", the events that followed the invasion demonstrated the limits and controversies of the prevailing practices of precautionary risk management for the governance of dangers. Insurgency and communal violence were treated as "unintended" side effects and responded to with more counter-insurgency measures, contributing to the intensification of violence and instability rather than reducing the security risk at the domestic as well as at the regional and global levels. Once again, the issue of responsibility and accountability remains problematic. While the risk producers have managed to get away with the consequences of their decisions and actions, the risk victims, the Iraqi people, are left to confront the persisting security and development challenges. In a BBC interview in September 2010, former UK Prime

Minister Tony Blair, who described the belief that Saddam Hussein was hiding weapons of mass destruction as an "understandable error" in his recently published memoirs, said how "desperately sorry" he felt for Iraqi victims but had no "regrets" for his decision to go to war, because, he argued, it was the right decision to make the world safer and he could never have foreseen the "nightmare that unfolded" after the invasion.

The prevailing representations of contemporary dangers as universal and catastrophic "emergencies" that need extraordinary preventive measures have led to the rise of "exceptionalism" as an instrument of security governance. This includes the deployment of "an array of illiberal policies and practices that are legitimated through claims about necessary exceptions to the norm" (Neal 2006: 31) such as the resurrection of "camps" (Agamben 2005) such as the Guantanamo Bay facility and the Abu Ghraib prison, the establishment of immigration detention centres, tightening border controls, implementing extra-legal surveillance, increasing restrictions on immigration policies, and the adoption of counter-terrorism legislation – all of which tend to undermine individual rights and freedoms. According to Italian philosopher Giorgio Agamben (2005), who argues that the "state of exception" or emergency has already become the "dominate paradigm of government in contemporary politics", what we are experiencing today is the "voluntary creation of a permanent state of emergency" in the context of a global war on terror.

Agamben structures his idea of the "state of exception as a paradigm of government" on a critique of Carl Schmitt's conception of the "state of exception" as a constitutive principle of political and social ordering on the basis of a "friend/enemy" distinction. For Schmitt, who is one of the most influential and also controversial political philosophers of the 20th century, the presence of the enemy is the essence of politics: the friend-foe distinction "to which political actions and motives can be reduced" (Schmitt 2007 [1932]: 26). It takes place in the "state of exception" that defines the functioning of the state and the law (ibid: 35). The "state of exception" or "emergency", however, is not a "construct" that can be applied to any situation of irregularity or moment of panic to enable state elites to further their interests, often through undermining civil liberties (Aradau and van Munster 2009). It rather refers to "a general concept in the theory of the state" that derives from a "gap" in the law which cannot be filled by jurists but only by a sovereign power (Schmitt 1985 [1922]). He suggests that no matter how detailed the law describing the complexities of everyday life, there will always be situations that fall outside the scope of law or "unpredictable times" because "the power of real life breaks through the crust of a mechanism that has become torpid with repetition" (ibid: 12). The potential forms that life may take or the situations that are impossible to anticipate in the legal system, he argues, may pose "a case of extreme peril, a danger to the existence of the state" (ibid: 6). What matters most at this "critical moment", according to Schmitt, is the definition of who makes the decision whether there is an "emergency" and what needs to be done about it or, as he puts it in his famous dictum, "Sovereign is he who decides on the exception" (ibid.). The "exception" from a Schmittian perspective therefore privileges the question of ''who decides'' over ''how to decide'' (Huysmans 2008) and requires the suspension of law, in which "the state remains, whereas law recedes" (Schmitt 1985 [1922]: 12). This situation, Schmitt emphasises, does not necessarily mean the violation of law or anarchy and chaos because when the state suspends the application of the constitution to defend itself or to preserve its political identity and territorial integrity, it does not cease to exist but still remains in force. It rather refers to a necessary but temporary arrangement decided on the basis of a right described in the constitution itself, rendering it a lawful and legitimate act. This political decision on the "exception" or "emergency", which removes all legal or normative procedural constraints upon political power in the necessity of facing the enemy, unifies "the people" with the political leadership (Huysmans 2008).

Agamben (2005) provides an historical account of the exercise of "emergency powers" by the executive in various Western democracies during the two world wars and the gradual transformation of these "provisional and exceptional" policy measures and practices into a "technique of government" in the aftermath of those wars. He rejects Schmitt's claim for the presence of a normative "gap" in the law that necessitates filling by the sovereign power. Firstly, he points to the subjectivity of deciding what makes a particular situation a necessity that requires an "exceptional" response. That is, "necessity entails a subjective judgment, and that obviously the only circumstances that are necessary and objective are those that are declared to be so" (ibid: 30). Secondly, by referring to Friedrich's point on the absence of institutional safeguards to ensure the temporary employment of emergency powers in the name of defending the constitution, he highlights the difficulty of defining and overcoming the danger of dictatorship through the exercise of constitutional emergency powers on a permanent basis. "Far from being a response to a normative lacuna", therefore, Agamben claims, "the state of exception appears as the opening of a fictitious lacuna in the order for the purpose of safeguarding the existence of the norm and its applicability to the normal situation" (ibid: 31). "Emergencies" are, in other words, likely to become the norm through a process of prolonged practices of "exceptional" measures and the perpetuation of conditions that are declared to be "emergency" or "exceptional" situations requiring new and more extraordinary responses. Expanded implementations of "exceptional" policy responses, especially in the context of an "endless war on terror" or a "global civil war", create a political environment in which the distinction between peace and war as well as between foreign and domestic disappears, and the exception or emergency becomes the norm (Agamben 2005). The separation between what is "normalcy" and what is an "exception" is eroded and the difference between the two realities becomes a matter of the degree of the shifting balance of power to the executive over time (Gross and Ni Aolain 2006). What were regarded as exceptional emergency actions in the past are now viewed as normal, routine and ordinary practices, in light of recent more extensive exercise of powers (ibid.). It should also be noted that the prolonged practices of the governance of insecurity through exceptional policies institutionalise fear as a constitutive principle of social ordering because emergency policies (Huysmans 2004: 338):

> are not simply about civil liberties, the legality of going to war, and the constitutional limits to strengthening executive-centred government. Since these political, legal and social contests strongly reiterate fear of the enemy they directly bear upon the extent to which one is structuring and possibly institutionalizing fear of the enemy as the organizing principle of politics in both national and international society. The question then becomes to what extent security responses that claim to aim at protecting freedom and equality are actually displacing freedom and equality with fear of the enemy as the central principle around which politics is organized.

The politics of fear and the construction of enemies are evidenced in the frequent representations of "failed" or "fragile" states as harbouring warlords and terrorists who are pursuing policies hostile to the "fundamental values and interests of the international society such as peace, stability, rule of law, freedom and democracy" (Yannis 2002). In this respect, former US President George Bush's well-known "with us or against us" speech in the wake of the Afghanistan intervention as part of the global "war on terror" best exemplifies the growing relevance of the friend-enemy distinction to the governance of terrorism: "Every nation, in every region, now has a decision to make. Either you are with us, or you are with the terrorists".

Australian Security and Strategic Planning under the Labor Government

Both the 2008 national security statement by Australia's former Prime Minister Kevin Rudd (Rudd 2008 hereinafter) and the subsequently released Defence White Paper entitled *Defending Australia in the Asia Pacific Century: Force 2030* (Department of Defence 2009) reflect the elements of prevailing perceptions of contemporary insecurity and its governance through the pursuit of "whole-of-government" policy responses. Australia's strategic objectives for the next two decades are in this respect defined on the basis of geographical priorities and concerns. As is self-evident in the title of the White Paper, the government's focus in regard to the pursuit of Australia's wider security interests is now back again on the Asia-Pacific region, perceived as the place where a chain of political, economic and military developments is shaping the course of future global order and shifting towards a multi-polar global order, in which US power will decline and China will rise. In this respect, the White Paper states that "it is not a principal task for the ADF [Australian Defence Force] to be generally prepared to deploy" to distant theatres such as the Middle East, Central Asia and Africa (ibid: 56). This suggests a retreat from the preceding Howard Government's "meaningful contributions" posture, defined as the deployment of Australian forces in US-led coalition operations to defend and promote Australia's "vital" strategic and broader security interests in distant places (Department of Defence 2005).

These shifts in policy orientation, however, do not necessarily indicate a radical departure in strategic guidance, which is still outlined in relation to the expansion of military capabilities to respond to regional and global uncertainties linked to power relativities and to maintain the alliance with the US and its involvement in the Asia-Pacific region as the backbone of Australia's security interests. The 2009 White Paper paints a picture similar to those provided in the previous defence documents produced in the last two decades. It starts by acknowledging the absence of a direct security threat in the form of armed attack that may come from other states or non-state actors but goes on to remark on the implications of strategic developments in the Asia-Pacific region, which are associated with the growing military capabilities of regional powers driven by their economic prosperity, for Australia's immediate and wider security interests (Department of Defence 2009: 49):

> The enduring reality of our strategic outlook is that Australia will most likely remain, by virtue of our geostrategic location, a secure country over the period to 2030. We are distant from traditional theatres of conflict

> between the major powers, and there is an absence of any serious, enduring disputes with our neighbours that could provide a motive for an attack... Australia has been a very secure country for many decades, in large measure because the wider Asia-Pacific region has enjoyed an unprecedented era of peace and stability underwritten by US strategic primacy. That order is being transformed as economic changes start to bring about changes in the distribution of strategic power. Risks resulting from escalating strategic competition could emerge quite unpredictably, and is a factor to be considered in our defence planning.

The primary policy instrument prescribed towards this aim is the pursuit of defence self-reliance, which has shaped Australian strategic guidance since the end of the Vietnam War. The government's geographically-focused defence self-reliance policy, informed by a broader hedging strategy against emerging risks and future uncertainties, is primarily based on sustaining the long-standing strategic alliance with the US and relying on its extended nuclear deterrence capabilities, while developing bilateral and multilateral defence and security partnerships with the neighbouring states. The White Paper also envisions the undertaking of the biggest defence restructuring since the end of the Second World War. The expansion of the nation's military capabilities, which involves the acquisition of new military equipment including long-range cruise missiles, submarines, joint strike fighter jets, frigates and air warfare destroyers, is estimated to cost around A$70 billion over 20 years, as reported in the media. The Rudd Government announced the introduction of a strategic reform package based on an "outputs-driven budget management model" aimed at creating savings of about A$20 billion; however, the funding issue still remains a big question.

In addition to its financial implications for tax-payers, the undertaking of such an ambitious military modernisation project has some other problematic aspects. Speculations and discussions around the questions of what kind of strategic environment is coming into existence since the collapse of the bipolar world system following the collapse of the Soviet Union and whether or not the US will be able sustain its dominant status or will be replaced by China, Russia, Japan or India in the near future have dominated the course of strategic thinking in the last two decades. And the balance of power in East Asia has shaped Australia's strategic guidance throughout the post-Cold-War period. What seems new in the current policy debates is a slightly more explicit identification of China's increasing military expenditure as a challenge to national and regional security and a response to it with more military measures, a manifestation of the "security dilemma". China has obviously been exercising a significant degree of influence in the Asia-Pacific region and playing a "*de facto* hegemonic role", as evidenced by its provision of "no strings attached" development assistance, military aid and loans to neighbouring countries, the joint production of military equipment and organisation of military exercises, participation in regional security forums and the production of defence memorandums of understanding (Dosch 2007). One might be forgiven for asking whether the perception of China's rising political and economic influence and military capabilities as a "cause for concern" for the other states in the region is based on convincing intelligence evidence which indicates the country's intention to use military force to pursue imperial or ideological interests.

According to the data provided by the Stockholm International Peace Research Institute (SIPRI 2010), world arms expenditure reached a new record in 2009, with US$1,531 billion being spent. China once again became the second biggest arms purchaser, estimated to have spent US$100 billion in current dollars. However, what is not much discussed in this regard is that China is not the only country that has continuously increased its military spending. In fact, the recent global financial crisis and economic recession seem to have had little impact on world military spending in 2009, which showed an increase of 6% in real terms from 2008 and an increase of 49% since 2000. The US spending of US$607 billion accounted for 43% of the world total in 2009. Ranking 14th in the SIPRI Yearbook, Australia spent US$19 billion, which was 8.5% higher in real terms than in 2008. As noted earlier, the acquisition of new military equipment is based on the perception of a shift in power in the Asia-Pacific region. The increasing military spending which seems to have given rise to a regional arms race may create new risks to national and regional security. According to the information on regional trends in military expenditures in the SIPRI Year Book, Asia and Oceania showed "the fastest real-terms increase with 8.9%".

The Rudd Government's "whole-of-government" approach to the governance of immediate and wider regional forms and sources of insecurity included the appointment of a National Security Adviser within the Prime Minister's Office to coordinate the government agencies involved in national security policy-making and facilitate the Commonwealth's work with the states and territories (Rudd 2008). The government's strategic framework also involved broadening the mandate and membership of the Secretaries Committee on National Security to encompass the full range of national security issues, and setting up a Crisis Coordination Centre to support government decision-making during crises situations (ibid.). In this respect, the analytical focus has so far been on operational aspects of this integrated security framework such as the problem of inter-agency coordination. What is not much discussed, however, as Haimeri (2009) points out, is the question of why "whole of government" has become the most appealing policy instrument throughout recent years. The answer can be found in the widening of strategic policy-making powers exercised by certain agencies of the executive branch of government that allows them to exert more influence over how policy issues are determined and by whom, and who should deal with them (ibid.). This has become apparent in the changing structure of the National Security Committee of Cabinet (NSCC) and the transformation of the organisational structure and role of the Australian Federal Police (AFP) in the post-September-11 period. The NSCC chaired by the Prime Minister established as a ministers-only organisation in 1996 under the Howard Government then became the "peak Commonwealth ministerial decision-making body on national security matters and the main vehicle for coordinating the Government's efforts in this regard", as Rudd reiterates in his 2008 national security statement. The AFP, whose budget rose from \$365 million in 2000-2001 to \$1.86 billion in 2005–2006, has significantly increased its power and influence both at home and in Australia's regional neighbourhood such as East Timor and the Solomon Islands, "without change in the level of ministerial control and parliamentary oversight and scrutiny" (Haigh 2008; see also Hameiri 2009).

Regional engagement is another significant component of this risk-based, integrated security framework that includes the provision of assistance to the Pacific island states. It is, however, not clear what kind of assistance is envisioned beyond a statement on the army's conduct of regional stabilisation and humanitarian relief operations. A policy emphasis is also placed upon border protection and surveillance to prevent the flow of refugees and illegal immigrants from reaching Australia. These policy measures, which aim to mitigate the destabilising effects of the intra-state conflicts which are expected to be the "most common form of conflict" during the period covered by the White Paper, are devised to effectively respond to instances of state "fragility", global demographic change and population movements, environmental and resource pressures, global public health risks and trans-national crime (Department of Defence 2009).

This emphasis on the tensions associated with the processes of globalisation also suggests what Ole Waever calls the "securitisation" (Waever 1995) of underdevelopment and population movements. This phenomenon became more apparent during the recent federal election campaign, centring on boat arrivals and immigration policies in the context of national security. The opposition leader, Tony Abbott, who was born overseas, called for tougher border security measures to "send a strong message to people smugglers that their cruel and callous trade in human cargo must stop". The new Labour leader Julia Gillard, whose parents moved from Wales in the 1960s in the Australian Government's "ten pound pom" migration scheme (assisted passage with adult migrants being charged a fare of only £10), rejected her predecessor Kevin Rudd's "big Australia" vision by emphasising the issues of sustainability, the capacity of the infrastructure and the availability of services in big cities to absorb population growth, and indicating her support for allowing entry to the "right kind of migrants".

The figures documented by the Parliamentary Library indicate that in 2010 134 boats with a total of about 6,879 people, including crew, arrived in Australia (Phillips and Sprinks 2011). Despite an overall increase in the number of unauthorised boat arrivals, this is still a small number compared to arrivals in European countries and the US (ibid.). Additionally, the majority of asylum applicants were still those who arrive in the country by plane with a valid visa (ibid.). It should also be noted that, despite the populist claims of asylum seekers trying to reach rich countries, the vast majority of refugees (between 75% and 90%) remain in their region of origin and constitute a serious burden for neighbouring countries (UNHCR 2009). In this context, the number of people seeking asylum in Western countries in 2009 remained 377,200, the same as in 2008. With 26,800 applications, Afghan nationals constituted the largest group of foreigners seeking asylum in developed countries. When this figure is compared to 1.7 million Afghan refugees already hosted in Pakistan and one million Afghans in Iran, "the notion that there is a flood of asylum seekers into richer countries is a myth", as the UNHCR chief points out (UNHCR 2010).

Conclusion: The Way Forward for Security

According to Robert Cox, one of the well-known theorists of the critical school of thought, "The Cold War has not ended, it has only become more unstable" (Cox 1994: 366). What we have been witnessing since the demise of the Soviet Union, Cox suggests, is not "a change from the Cold War but a change in the Cold War" (ibid.). The continuing recourse to armaments and other already discredited military solutions to cope with a range of dangers perceived to be emanating from the so-called "failed" or "fragile" states illustrates the search for a "new other", indicating the persistence of the Cold War mentality that continues to shape strategic thinking and action today. The "world on fire" image (Chua 2003) dominates the current notions of insecurity. Although the number of armed conflicts almost halved by 2003 from a peak in 1992 (Human Security Centre 2005), this is not mentioned in the media or in policy circles, let alone being studied by the research community in detail. Instead, the focus has been on the governance of "emergencies" such as refugees, illegal immigrants and terrorists by pursuing preventive risk management measures such as border patrolling, surveillance, and regional and global military operations. These policy responses, which provoke fear of the enemy in society, actually tend to manufacture new forms of insecurity that are usually treated as "unintended side effects" with no talk of responsibility and accountability. However, risk calculus, which is about making decisions on containing or controlling future catastrophes, is not an objective process, as Beck argues, but is essentially a power-driven process in which some actors and sectors exercise a greater capacity to define risks for "others" and to benefit from the global production of risks. Furthermore, the governance of insecurity and its future uncertain and possibly catastrophic consequences through more "emergency" or "exceptional" policy responses tends to produce the conditions of a permanent emergency that Agamben warns against.

What we need, therefore, is to change the mindset in understanding contemporary insecurities towards a more balanced understanding of globalisation and its diverging effects on security in different parts of the world. This requires examining the processes of economic globalisation and acknowledging the structural socio-political and economic conditions of "fragility" or "failure" in some societies and "success" or "strength" in others, rather than focusing on "supposed symptoms of state failure" such as terrorism (Bilgin and Morton 2007). This also entails the pursuit of a unifying rather than a divisive perspective on a world that is composed of so-called zones of stability and prosperity surrounded by zones of conflict, thereby abandoning in the process what Duffield (2001) calls "'their' underdevelopment is 'our' insecurity" framework. Establishing some, if not full, responsibility and accountability rather than relying on the language of the universal, destructive and unpredictable character of contemporary security risks constitutes another aspect of this change. Last but not least, it requires balancing policy responses with social peace, cohesion and democracy to respond effectively to public expectations such as social security and welfare needs. In a country that prides itself on upholding basic rights, freedoms and development needs for all its citizens, the success of Australia's security policy can be better analysed to the extent that it aligns with this framework.

References

Agamben, Giorgio. 2005. *The state of exception*, trans. Kevin Attell. Chicago, London: The University of Chicago Press.

Aradau, Claudia and Rens van Munster. 2009. Exceptionalism and the "war on terror": Criminology meets international relations. *British Journal of Criminology* 49 (5): 686–701.

Beck, Ulrich. 1992. *Risk society: Towards a new modernity*. London: Sage.

—. 1999. *World risk society*. Malden, Mass: Polity Press.

—. 2006. Living in the world risk society. *Economy and Society* 35 (3): 329–345.

Bilgin, Pinar. 2003. Individual and societal dimensions of security. *International Studies Review* 5 (2): 203–222.

Bilgin, Pinar and Adam David Morton. 2007. Rethinking state failure: The political economy of security. In *State failure revisited I: Globalization of security and neighborhood effects*, eds Daniel Lambach and Tobias Debiel. Institute for Development and Peace (INEF) Report No. 87: 7–31.

Bloomfield, David and Ben Reilly. 1998. The changing nature of conflict and conflict management. In *Democracy and deep-rooted conflict: Options for negotiators*, eds Peter Harris and Ben Reilly. International Institute for Democracy and Electoral Assistance (IDEA) Handbook Series (Stockholm: IDEA): 7–28.

Boutros-Ghali, Boutros. 1992. *An agenda for peace: Preventive diplomacy, peacemaking and peace-keeping*. New York: United Nations.

British Department for International Development (DFID). 2005. *Why we need to work more effectively in fragile states*. London: DFID.

Chandler, David. 2008. Human security: The dog that didn't bark. *Security Dialogue* 39 (4): 427–438.

Chua, Amy. 2004. *World on fire: How exporting free market democracy breeds ethnic hatred and global instability*. New York: Anchor.

Cox, Robert. 1994. The forum: Hegemony and social change. *Mershon International Studies Review* 38 (2): 366–7.

Department of Defence. 2005. *Australia's national security: A defence update*. Canberra: Department of Defence.

—. 2009. *Defending Australia in the Asia Pacific century: Force 2030*. Canberra: Department of Defence.

Dosch, Jorn. 2007. Managing security in ASEAN-China relations: Liberal peace of hegemonic stability. *Asian Perspective* 31 (1): 209–236.

Duffield, Mark. 1997. NGO relief in war zones: Towards an analysis of the new aid paradigm. *Third World Quarterly* 18 (3): 527–542.

—. 2001. *Global governance and the new wars.* London and New York: Zed Books.

Evans, Michael. 2007. Towards an Australian national security strategy: A conceptual analysis. *Security Challenges* 3 (4): 113–130.

Fukuyama, Francis. 2004. *State-building: Governance and world order in the 21st century.* Ithaca, NY: Cornell University Press.

Gross, Oren and Fionnuala Ni Aolain. 2006. *Law in times of crisis: Emergency powers in theory and practice.* Cambridge, NY: Cambridge University Press.

Haigh, Bruce. 2008. The paramilitary wing of the AFP. *On line opinion.* http://www.onlineopinion.com.au/view.asp?article=7033 (accessed 3 September 2010).

Hameiri, Shahar. 2009. Governing disorder: The Australian Federal Police and Australia's new regional frontier. *The Pacific Review* 22 (5): 549–74.

Hataley, T. S. and Kim Richard Nossal. 2004. The limits of the human security agenda: The case of Canada's response to the Timor crisis. *Global Change, Peace and Security* 16 (1): 5–17.

Helman, Gerald B. and Steven R. Ratner. 1992–3. Saving failed states. *Foreign Policy* 89: 3–20.

Human Security Centre. 2005. *Human security report 2005: War and peace in the 21st century.* Vancouver: Human Security Centre.

Huysmans, Jef. 2004. Minding exceptions: Politics of insecurity and liberal democracy. *Contemporary Political Theory* 3 (3): 321–41.

—. 2008. The jargon of exception: On Schmitt, Agamben and the absence of political society. *International Political Sociology* 2 (2): 165–183.

Kaldor, Mary. 1999. *New and old wars: Organised violence in a global era.* Cambridge: Polity Press.

Milliken, Jennifer and Keith Krause. 2002. State failure, state collapse and state reconstruction: Concepts, lessons and strategies. *Development and Change* 33 (5): 753–774.

Neal, Andrew W. 2006. Foucault in Guantanamo: Towards an archaeology of the exception. *Security Dialogue* 37 (1): 31–46.

Nossal, Kim Richard. 1995. Seeing things? The adornment of "security" in Australia and Canada. *Australian Journal of International Affairs* 49 (1): 33–47.

Organisation for Economic Co-operation and Development and the Development Assistance Committee (OECD/DAC). 2009. Concepts and dilemmas of state building in fragile situations. *OECD Journal on Development* 9 (3): 64–152.

Paris, Roland. 2001. Human security: Paradigm shift or hot air? *International Security* 26 (2): 87–102.

Phillips, Janet and Harriet Spinks. 2011. *Boat arrivals in Australia since 1976: Background note.* Canberra: Parliament of Australia.

Rasmussen, Mikkel Vedby. 2006. *The risk society at war: Terror, technology and strategy in the twenty-first century.* Cambridge University Press.

Rotberg, Robert I. 2003a. Failed states, collapsed states, weak states: Causes and indicators. In *When states fail: Causes and consequences*, ed. Robert I. Rotberg. Washington D.C: Brookings Institution Press.

—. 2003b. State failure and state weakness in a time of terror. In *When states fail: Causes and consequences*, ed. Robert I. Rotberg, 1–25. Washington D.C: Brookings Institution Press.

Rudd, Kevin. 2008. *The first national security statement to the Australian Parliament: Address by the Prime Minister of Australia, the Hon. Kevin Rudd MP*, 4 December 2008. Canberra.

Schmitt, Carl. 1985 (1922). *Political theology: Four chapters on the concept of sovereignty*, trans. George Schwab. Cambridge: MIT Press.

—. 2007 (1932). *The concept of the political*, trans. and introduction George Schwab, foreword Tracy B. Strong and annotated Leo Straus. Chicago, London: The University of Chicago Press.

Stockholm International Peace Research Institute (SIPRI). 2010. *SIPRI yearbook 2010: Armaments, disarmament and international security.* Oxford; New York: Oxford University Press.

United Nations Development Programme (UNDP). 1994. *Human development report: New dimensions of human security.* New York: Oxford University Press.

United Nations High Commissioner for Refugees (UNHCR). 2009. *2008 global trends: Refugees, asylum-seekers, returnees, internally displaced and stateless persons.* UNHCR.

—. 2010. *Asylum levels and trends in industrialized countries 2009: Statistical overview of asylum applications lodged in Europe and selected non-European countries.* UNHCR.

Waever, Ole. 1995. Securitization and desecuritization. In *On security*, ed. Ronnie D. Lipschutz, 46–86. New York: Columbia University Press.

Walt, Stephen W. 1991. The renaissance of security studies. *International Studies Quarterly* 35: 211–239.

Yannis, Alexandros. 2002. State collapse and its implications for peace-building and reconstruction. *Development and Change* 33 (5): 817–835.

CHAPTER FIVE

AUSTRALIA'S WAR ON TERRORISM: IMPACT ON AUSTRALIAN MUSLIM COMMUNITIES*

TAHMINA RASHID

> Crisis occurs when the social formation can no longer be reproduced on the basis of the pre-existing system of social relations.
> —Stuart Hall

> The identity a person takes on will be profoundly shaped by the ways in which others identify and react to him or her.
> —Akers 1997: 101

> It was easy for judges of constitutional courts to accord basic rights to popular minorities and individuals. The real test came when they were asked to accord the same rights to unpopular minorities and individuals.
> —Sheller Report: 41

The debates and legislation since 2001 around the themes of "counter terrorism", "war against terrorism" and "war on terrorism" in Australia have generated complex scenarios, leading to fear and the creation of Otherness (us versus them). Mainstream debates on counter terrorism have created fear among mainstream society of Muslims as the threat, simultaneously creating fear of the state among Muslims. Muslim communities feel that they are criminalised through legislation which openly doubts their allegiance to Australia and suspects criminal intent.

Public discourses have given an impression to Muslim communities that Muslims have the sole responsibility of countering terrorism in Australia and have to provide information on potential suspects and

---

* I have consciously used the term "Muslim communities" rather than "Muslim community" to highlight the fact that Australian Muslims are not a homogenous group.

suspicious activities in their communities. Muslims of Middle Eastern origin became a "fifth column"; however, Pakistani and Indian Muslims were also eventually labelled as potential terrorists, in dire need of scrutiny by all. Some of these vociferous negative discourses and legislative measures have created an atmosphere of "guilt by association", justifying curtailing civil liberties in the name of countering terrorism. Civil liberties advocates have criticised these measures as potential tools for victimisation on a number of political grounds. Muslim communities have experienced victimisation ever since these discourses entered the public debate. Irrespective of the reality of their fears, because of being labelled "potential terrorists", "un-Australian", "guilty by association", "Other", "citizens with suspect allegiance" and "guilty until proven innocent", Muslims are feeling the impact on their sense of belonging and Australian identity. Muslim women have to confront an additional factor if they choose to wear headscarves. This chapter explores these issues from the perspective of migrants as well as Australian-born Muslim youth.

The Context: Australian Muslims

In Australia, general hysteria about the growing number of Muslim migrants and asylum seekers and the growth rate of the Muslim population has failed to take into account the actual statistics. We frequently hear unqualified comments regarding the need to fear or loathe a growing minority group, therefore it is vital to look at the local context before considering the issues surrounding counter-terrorism, war against/on terrorism and the role Muslims ought or ought not to play in these debates. Australian Muslims are a small minority in Australia, less than 2% of the total population. Census data (2006) indicates that since 2001 the largest groups of arrivals have been from England, New Zealand, China, India and South Africa, and that Christianity is the most common religion (46.1% of the immigrants during this period). According to the 2006 census data, the Australian Muslim population is 1.7% (340,400) of the total Australian population. Of these, 58.5% (199,070) were born overseas and 37.9% (128,904) were born in Australia. The table below gives more details on age group and gender, highlighting the large proportion below the age of 24.

Age and Gender of Muslims in Australia – 2006 Census

Age	Male	Female
0-14	52,346	49,552
15-24	32,943	31,007
25-44	59,488	54,580
45-64	27,437	22,826
65+	5,536	4,669

Source: 2006 Census of Population and Housing (Australian Bureau of Statistics)

Looking at the segregated data on the basis of Muslims born in Australia and in other parts of the world, we see the great diversity in ethnic origins and also the percentage of young people born in Australia.

Australian Muslims – Birthplace

Birthplace	Percentage	Birthplace	Percentage
Australia	37.9	Bangladesh	3.9
Lebanon	8.9	Iraq	2.9
Turkey	6.8	Indonesia	2.5
Afghanistan	4.7	Bosnia & Herzegovina	2.2
Pakistan	4.1	Iran	2.1

Source: 2006 Census of Population and Housing (Australian Bureau of Statistics)

Nearly 50% of the Australian Muslims live in NSW, followed by Victoria and WA. Although predominantly stereotyped as Middle Eastern, census data gives a different account of these diverse communities. The table above shows that all Muslims are neither Arabs nor Middle Eastern, and also come from South and Central Asia as well as Indonesia. One interesting feature about Australian Muslims is their placement in popular imagination and official discourses. Unlike other ethno-religious groups, Muslims are neither considered a race like the Jewish people, based on shared faith and thus unified as a group that qualifies for protection under anti-racial legislation (Malik 2009), nor is the ethnic-cultural diversity of Muslims recognised, thus homogenising them as a single group, unifying all diversity under the banner of religion and ignoring the diversity between various sects as practised by Australian Muslim communities. Due to the variances in state and federal legislation, Muslim communities' experiences vary based on their location. Muslims living in Victoria have protection under the Racial and Religious Tolerance Act (2002), while those living in South Australia have no such protection (Spalek 2007: 190).

It has been established through various studies that social relations between Muslim communities and mainstream Australia changed dramatically following the events of September 11, 2001. In response to these events, the Howard regime introduced a range of legislative measure to deal with any potential threats of terrorism in Australia in addition to joining the US "War on Terrorism". It could be argued that joining the US alliance was a foreign policy move to enhance Australia's role in global politics; however, it had long-term implications for domestic politics as well as social cohesion. Successive regimes have tried to connect or disconnect Australian participation in the US-led alliance with an increased security threat to Australia. Without considering the wisdom of the Howard era and its foreign policy agenda, one can analyse the language and rhetoric of government discourses and the manner in which they transformed media and popular discourses about Australian Muslim communities.

In response to the threat envisioned by the Howard regime, Australia introduced over 40 pieces of legislation to counter potential terrorism. The language and statements of these legislative measures have labelled Muslim communities "designated community of interest". Before going into further details on the impact of these measures on Muslim communities, I would like to highlight the power of such labelling and framing, and the manner in which it generates fear not only among the general public but also among Muslim communities, leading to a breakdown in social cohesion. Such a situation can negatively impact on a sense of belonging and also increase a sense of "Otherness" on both sides. I would like to extrapolate the concept of framing and labelling employed by Moncrieffe (2007) in a different context. She suggests that:

> Labelling is pervasive and inevitable… regulates social interactions; it helps us to define the terms on which we relate to 'others'… is instrumental for policy, including managing the allocation and distribution of scarce resources.

Her explanation of how framing refers to our understanding of issues and their representation in policy discourses, and how labelling refers to naming/categorising people is relevant to the context under discussion as a determining factor in engaging with Muslim communities in Australia. Moncrieffe demonstrates that by labelling communities, policy makers and also non-state actors such as media, political leadership and various communities "influence how particular issues and categories of people are regarded and treated" (Moncrieffe 2007: 2), thus establishing a relationship of power through labelling and framing with little accountability for any negative outcomes. There are three central elements in framing and labelling processes: the state, non-state actors and the media (talkback radio, print and electronic media and social media). The state plays a central and hegemonic role in labelling that is reflected in the language employed in various legislative measures, policy speeches and documents related to Australia's "war on terrorism".

It needs to be highlighted that the initial global response to the events of September 11, 2001, constructed a discourse through carefully constructed language that was aligned with US foreign policy. This justified state violence through counter-terrorism policies and normalised violence as a foreign policy instrument, and at the same time silenced criticism and narrowed the concepts of national identity. The meta-narrative of terrorism is perfectly aligned with orientalist and neo-colonial mindsets, on a mission to civilise the barbarians who mindlessly kill and have no respect for human life. It became a war to save "our way of life" and "our values", thus making the enemy a threat that was interpreted by political leadership, opinion makers and think-tanks as threat not only to democracy and freedom but also to modernisation and globalisation. Combined with the stereotypical depiction of various Muslim groups by the media, a pariah from within was created that symbolised the enemy. Muslim women wearing hijab were a perfect fit for this anti-modernity symbolism and provided an instant connection between the criminals involved in the September 11, 2001, attacks and Muslim communities in Australia. This not only obscured the political grievances of any groups involved but focused on their inhumanity and justified our partnership in the US military invasion of Iraq and Afghanistan, thus creating a jingoistic national identity. This nationalistic identity or imagined political community became a boundary marker and hastened a process of "Othering" – us and them, insiders and outsiders, modern and anti-modern, citizens and immigrants – and the Other became a focal point of defining "us". The new identity discourse not only had a political and nationalistic but also a theological agenda, bringing the morality or immorality of various actors into the political arena. It has categorised Muslim communities according to faith only, homogenising their racial, ethnic, linguistic and sectarian differences.

These new categories of events and enemies have been generated in a vacuum, devoid of historical context, conspicuously omitting the political dimension of terrorism and depoliticising counter-terrorism policies. Jackson (2005: 181) argues that such depoliticising does politicise public discourses and destroys the moral consensus to legitimise large-scale political violence. He insists that, "Once a society embraces these new political narratives, once it venerates its grievances and truly hates and fears an enemy 'other', public and political morality is quickly lost in the maze of national security expediencies". Any war casualty is defined in terms of the brutality of the enemy, masking the logic behind military intervention and our involvement without due domestic political consensus. These discourses delegitimised domestic political opposition to joining the US alliance, as opposition could be labelled unpatriotic.

During the Howard regime, the usage of political language and the reaffirmation of Australia's Judeo-Christian and British heritage and assertions of "not being obsessed with diversity" (Michael 2009: 50) had a profound impact on ethnically diverse immigrant communities, including Muslims. Peter Costello lashed out at terrorism, unifying terrorists, Muslims and misguided multiculturalism, during his ambitious skirmish for political leadership. Alexander Downer frequently made distinctions between Western moderation and extreme Islam/terrorism. In one of his speeches he stated that:

> Australia faces a serious threat from international terrorism and we must prepare for this reality. As a Western democratic country, our values of peace, religious freedom, liberty and tolerance put us squarely in the terrorists' sights. Contemporary terrorism differs from any threat previously faced by Australia. This scourge compromises our way of life and we cannot ignore or hide from it.

Close analysis of the rhetoric employed by the Howard regime through statements, policy documents and legislative pieces show how Muslims are framed and labelled. Political leadership has used the power to frame and label Australian Muslim communities as a homogenised group of people that pose "potential threat" to Australian national security and hence the Australian people. This framing of Australian Muslims as "potential threat" has labelled them as the "Other" – not one of us but the other who can potentially harm "unified us". Such fears lead to heightened security and denial of rights to non-citizens, which can potentially limit the rights of citizens as well. Jackson suggests that:

> The creation of widespread moral panic can lead to ordinary citizens acting as the primary agents of censure themselves, both in terms of self-censorship (choosing to withhold their doubts and disagreements in public discourse) and the censorship of others (expressing disapproval when confronted with dissenting or "disloyal" opinion in others).
> (Jackson 2005: 116)

The relationship of power in the framing and labelling process has little impact on policy makers yet they are able to exercise this power without much accountability or public scrutiny. In Australia, criticism by civil liberty groups pushed the policy makers to acknowledge the flaws in the legislative process, yet the politicians hastened to approve the legislation with a promise of a later review. This short-sighted callousness on the part of the policy makers confounds rational examination by any standard, yet the bill was passed with a majority vote as none of the political parties dared to question the wisdom of passing flawed legislation. Civil liberty groups opposed the measures and highlighted the future implications on the rights of citizens and non-citizens in the absence of appropriate safeguards, yet the political parties were united in their support for hastening the process to participate in the global war on terrorism locally. Jackson (2005: 183–4) is of the view that:

> Apart from destabilizing society's moral consensus, the discourse and practice of counter-terrorism inevitably leads to the delegitimisation of dissent and the narrowing of the discursive space for political debate. In large part, this is because fighting the "enemy within" requires strict social discipline, patriotism, conformity, informers, loyalty pledges and the bifurcation of national life; it requires clear lines between good and evil, between self and other, citizen and foreigner, inside and outside – all of which is the antithesis of a healthy politics. The moral taxonomy of the language of good versus evil is by definition incompatible with democratic politics because it undermines the possibility of a loyal opposition.

Civil libertarians' insistence on adding a sunset clause gave these laws a ten-year span of life (to expire in 2016). The Opposition leader even suggested "locking down Lakemba" after ASIO raids and arrests of potential terrorists in November 2005 in Sydney. Such careless remarks make all Muslims responsible for these criminal acts (Pollak 2006). Chesney (2003: 1414) argues that in a crisis situation, "fear may cause decision makers either to overestimate the scope of the security threat, to underestimate the value of the civil liberties at stake, or both", suggesting that fear may lead to a moral panic. A moral panic exaggerates the perceptions of threat, resulting in collective hostility towards a community labelled as the outsiders – a pattern of ethnic and religious profiling. The politics of fear before the 2004 Australian federal election revealed the alarmist nature of national politics, labelling Muslims as the definitional element at the very core of the terrorist threat to the nation.

The political leadership's panicked patriotic response and the urgency of passing counter-terrorism laws denied the right to oppose the legislation and also any opportunity of frank public discussion. The Howard regime won the election by raising fears about Australian national security after September 11, 2001, and tried to invoke Islamophobia during the 2006 election by raising security concerns after the case of an Indian doctor working in Queensland who was linked to a Glasgow bomber made headlines. Jackson (2005: 188) is of the view that:

> The nature of the political discourse that has prevented the consideration of alternative paradigms and approaches to counter-terrorism, the inbuilt logic of the language, and the privileging of only certain kinds of knowledge, has circumvented the kind of in-depth, rigorous and informed debate that a complex political challenge such as terrorism requires.

Once the moral panic was produced at the policy-making level, the media contributed with impunity in escalating fear in the popular imagination. Partial stories in the media contributed to the grand narrative about Muslims in Australia by mutilating the socio-historical context, reallocating legitimate public space and legitimising a variance in the distribution of social, economic and political power. The substantive power of the media has been overlooked, relegated to a few sporadic comments on talkback radio and raising another question regarding agency: "who can speak and whose voices be heard and count?" Yet the motives for such framing and labelling in the public/media discourses have not been challenged. These motives may lead to unanticipated outcomes, stigmatising Muslim communities and sustaining unwanted outcomes. Media representations create the hegemonies of public discourse on Muslim communities, invalidating other possible and valid representations in the public sphere (Pickering 2007).

Sensational headlines such as "Muslims are refusing to give national security authorities counter-terrorism tip-offs" (Kerbaj 2007) further break down the trust between communities. There is anxiety and fear among Muslim communities due to the hype created by the media and the targeting of people who "look like Muslims", homogenising all as one group of people who must have shared views on religion, culture and nationhood. Some media suggestions that all Muslims want the implementation of *Shariah* laws in Australia are not supported by evidence, nor is that aim supported by all Muslims, who belong to various sects and thus make different legal interpretations. Despite critical voices of reason talking about implications for civil liberties, the mainstream media followed the official government line and reproduced the same discourse. The corporatisation of the media and the state monopoly of war news pushed the media to toe the official policy line. Fears raised by

Muslim communities have been sidelined, as these communities lack agency in mainstream media.

Unlike the US, Australia is not an extremely religious country, yet the policies have employed religious narratives to describe terrorists and to justify counter-terrorism policies, asking Muslim communities to pledge their loyalty to their adopted country, assuming that they are all immigrants and subscribers to terrorist ideology. The Australian Islamist Monitor, a radical anti-Islamic group, criticised PAAT 2006 for failing to address the "profound theological and philosophical divide between Australian society and Islamic culture". Such assertions categorise all Muslims as the same, practising one Islamic culture and thus being the "Other". Such minority views demonstrate the fear-mongering that gives Muslims a blanket homogenous identity, demands the slashing of government funding for Islamic schools, suggests a ban on Muslim immigration and proposes that Muslims be required to sign a statement repudiating allegiance to their country of origin (laws, culture, umma) and repudiating those parts of *Quran* that are contrary to Australian laws. Other proposals by extreme minority groups are to require all Muslims who contest elections to swear allegiance to the Queen and to monitor the preaching in mosques. Such views resonate in the talkback radio conversations where comments are inflamed by fear about threats to "our way of life". Fred Nile, Alan Jones and like-minded public figures continue to suggest that Muslims and Islam are incompatible with the "Australian way of life".

Non-state actors label Muslim communities with various kinds of signifiers, yet even when used for noble purposes these labels mark the communities as the "Other" and may involve questionable methods and strategies leading to negative impacts and unanticipated/unintended consequences. As a result of such labelling, there is growing public support for the detention of terror suspects without charge, life imprisonment for supporting a terrorist organisation and seven years of imprisonment for supporting insurgencies where Australian troops are deployed (Veit 2005: 36). Ironically, public paranoia and support for extreme punitive measures is in total contrast to the very rights and freedoms valued by society and in danger of being eroded due to terrorist acts.

Social Cohesion and Responsibilities of Muslim Communities and Citizens

Successive Australian regimes have dealt with immigration, race relations, multiculturalism and ethnic diversity in different ways. Their policies have been reflected through the political leadership's language, such as diversity, multiculturalism and citizenship, as well as resource allocation for services for newly arrived migrants. Despite these variations in services as well as in the opportunities available, these citizens are expected to assimilate yet one can only be flabbergasted about the principles for gauging their assimilation. At the same time, the state and the wider society either ignore or fail to comprehend the inequality and social deprivation among most migrant communities. A large percentage (43%) of Australian Muslims (Census data 2001) earn less than $200 per week compared to the national average of 27%. State funding for community projects, especially related to Imams' education, services for women (shelters for the victims of domestic violence and human rights education), aged care, refugees and asylum seekers, and educational opportunities is very limited. The discussions through the Muslim Community Reference Group (MCRG) established during the Howard era have not led to significant changes or increased agency for Muslim communities. This selective engagement with the state produced a "legitimate Muslim identity", adding another layer of exclusion for those who had already been excluded from the process because of being labelled as radical. Thus the engagement between the state and Muslim communities has been based on exclusion rather than inclusion.

The assumption than any traditional/orthodox Muslim is a potential terrorist and therefore outside the national engagement process is not just naïve but dangerous as it widens the space for proponents of violence in the name of religion. Spalek (2007: 198) argues that this assumption ignores the multiplicity of identity construction, highlighting the fluidity of identities – national/territorial and religious/philosophical. Ironically these dual and fluid identities are sanctioned for communities with generational connections with Europe and other parts of the globe but questioned suspiciously when it comes to Muslim communities. Such denial further limits the likelihood of participation in the processes for setting the agendas for communities' engagement with the state that has homogenised Muslim communities as one. Spalek (2007: 201) raises a grave concern regarding the appropriateness of the state's involvement in the "internal affairs and structures of a religious community in a secular nation that believes in the separation between "church" and state. He further questions:

> whether governments' willingness to be involved in such discussions are illustrative of the structures and practices which result in oppression experienced by many Muslims in both the UK and Australia... most governments in Western secular democratic countries would be loathe to interfere in the internal structures and affairs of any other "mainstream" religion even where there was a slight potential of inappropriate behaviour on the part of "clergy" or religious teachers... Hence, the suspicion that some imams or religious teachers might encourage acts of terrorism is not, in our opinion, adequate reasons for governments to do away with the notion of a division between "church" and state without due public and intellectual discussion of this.

Howard's attempts to engage Muslims through the MRCG (Muslim Community Reference Group) and sub-groups failed to engage these communities as citizens with the state; they rather reinforced the divide not merely between Muslim communities and mainstream society but within the Muslim communities. The Australian Government endeavoured to create artificial cohesion and its failure to recognise the diversity within the communities requires forging a "new Muslim identity" (Bergin 2007: 15). The handpicked MRCG members neither had the mandate of the communities nor were they representatives of all ethnic, racial, linguistic and sectarian cleavages. This government attempt to include citizens as legitimate representatives on the state's own terms excluded those who were not perceived as legitimate or worthy of inclusion. Ironically, the regime intended to engage these communities as Australian citizens by labelling them as the Other. Muslim communities' responsibilities as active citizens have been framed through counter-terrorism legislation, creating fear of permanent surveillance within the community as well as from homeland security agencies. Muslim communities view these efforts with suspicion as agendas are set by the regime and there is little room for opposing the existing policies. Les Luck, Ambassador for Counter-Terrorism, DFAT, stated that:

> In this struggle, our greatest allies will be those mainstream Muslims and moderate Muslim leaders and politicians best placed to assert orthodox values in the face of fanaticism and stare down terrorist sympathisers.

Assumptions regarding community surveillance as the responsibility of Australian Muslim citizens (Bergin 2007) can lead to self-censorship and self-denial of their rights as citizens for legitimate political opposition to the policies of any government. Increasingly the state has assumed the role of a regulator and is expected to regulate religion through various measures. Such demands also assume that it is the responsibility of Muslim communities alone to deter any potential terrorist threat to Australia, as if any such threat is not a threat to Australian Muslim communities.

Another related factor is the prevailing notion of guilt by association replacing the presumption of innocence until proven guilty. "Guilty by association" may be aimed to discourage the formation of groups associating for criminal purposes, yet the secrecy associated with the process in respect to access to information and legal avenues for justice may result in denial of due process of law. In the absence of a clear understanding of permissible and impermissible limits of criminalised association, social engagement with community members may be complicated if any associates are found to be linked with the members of an association later added to the proscribed list.

Muslim communities have a range of views on anti-terrorism legislation, from inward-looking apologists to staunch opponents who view these laws as creating tensions rather than solutions. This range of views can be seen in the responses to the 2010 White Paper on Counter-Terrorism, blaming the Australian Government for targeting Muslims and being part of the Western alliance against the Muslim world. It has to be recognised that radical groups such as Hizb-ut-Tahrir (even though not a proscribed organisation in Australia) would criticise Australian laws and policies on counter-terrorism on different grounds than the large majority of Muslims who wish to participate in the nationhood project as citizens and not as the "Other" or a special category assigned by the state. It could reasonably be argued that there is a need to monitor these radical groups, as would be expected by the Muslim communities, but the surveillance and policing responsibility could not be taken without formally assigning a proscribed status.

The state needs to recognise the need for educating communities (not just Muslim communities) about the laws and implications associated with various aspects, especially when the legislation takes previous associations into account. A 2007 report (Australia Deliberates) concluded that the level of education among Australians was directly linked to their perceptions about Muslims and a higher level of education among respondents was linked to an accommodating attitude towards diversity and an awareness of the historical and political context of various global events. Refugees and asylum seekers coming from different conflict zones may open new avenues of discrimination under new interpretations of "association". Newly arrived migrants and asylum seekers (irrespective of their religion) figure relatively highly in abusive experiences at the hands of law-enforcing agencies, thus raising real fears about preventive detention that only requires the approval of a senior police officer as opposed to questioning detention that requires approval from DG ASIO. Mark Burgess, chief executive of the Police Federation of Australia, has indicated that:

> What we're concerned about is that intelligence generally will identify the type of person who might be under suspicion for a terrorist attack. That person, by and large, are not going to be 60-year-old women and 70-year-old men. Unfortunately, more often than not, the profile will be young men of Middle Eastern appearance… We're just saying to the Government they need to take into account the concerns that we're raising. It's inevitable that there will be unintended consequences of this legislation and we just want to make sure that there is some protection for police officers… Obviously there's education programs etc, but at the end of the day, we've got to understand that police officers are the people at the front line. Police officers are the people that have actually got to use these laws. We just want to make sure that the legislators understand that there could be unintended consequences and we want to make sure that police are protected.
> (Roy 2005)

These new powers given to police officers and ASIO have also raised concerns regarding "stop and search" and over-policing along racial and religious lines. There are numerous misunderstandings especially regarding association outside the place of prayer that are not covered under these laws yet form part of daily community life. The Australian Muslim Civil Rights Advocacy Network (2006) has highlighted these issues, indicating that social occasions such as weddings, funerals, and various cultural and religious festivals are not covered under these laws. It is not easy to dismiss these fears, especially when ethnic and religious profiling of Muslims has become part of our public discourse and such criminalisation has been subtly institutionalised. Recent ASIO raids on the offices of a (not proscribed) Kurdish organisation in Melbourne have heightened fears among the communities that these laws can be used to deny the human rights available to other Australian citizens. There are also fears regarding sedition laws that may limit freedom of expression or speaking out against injustice, especially if what is said does not comply with Australian foreign policy. The application of these laws may result in curbing any political opposition by civil rights groups to government policies and eroding the foundations of liberal democracy. Notwithstanding the politics of diversity and multiculturalism, the fragile social cohesiveness seems to be further fracturing due to such policies and there is neither a vision for the mechanisms of achieving social cohesion nor is there any leadership or vision for future dialogue between the state and Muslim communities. Any incident can potentially accelerate the process of complete breakdown of this relationship, further necessitating a meaningful engagement.

Engagement with Australian Muslim Women and Youth

The prevailing public discourses are patriarchal, both in terms of the military invasion in Afghanistan (rescuing women from the oppression of the Taliban) and labelling veil/hijab as a sign of male oppression in the Australian context. This effectively terms Muslim women as voiceless citizens not only in the Muslim world but also in Australia, whose rescue is the responsibility of modern civilised "us". Their voices are equally sidelined and silenced by patriarchal Muslim men (as claimed by the prevailing counter-terrorism discourse) and the modern state.

Muslim women who decide to wear the burka/veil either for religious reasons or to mark their identity are the chosen targets. Advocates of freedom of expression fail to see the hypocrisy when they argue for the protection of their right to criticise Islam and its associated rituals or practices yet at the same time deny the same rights to Muslim women. The argument used by various non-state actors that the veil is a signifier is groundless because not all Australian Muslim women wear the veil or wear it for the same reasons. For Muslim women, the veil may not be the prime signifier determining the views of individuals and communities on matters related to terrorism, as indicated in popular debates and perceptions.

For young Australian Muslims, of whom around 37% are born here, Australia is their home, the only place they identify with. For these young men and women, identifying themselves as the "Other" or an "Outsider" will have a different meaning from a first-generation migrant. Listening to some minority views through talkback radio or other media, with suggestions "to go back where you come from" can only lead to provocation, yet the question remains: where to go from home? Moncrieffe (2007: 4) is of the view that such negative labelling produced through action (state; non-state actors; media) and inaction (state) leads to stigmatised communities, especially youth who may accept and even uphold the meanings attached to this label. This negative label questions young people's sense of belonging, allegiance and loyalty as Australian citizens. Australian Muslim communities raise concerns that such labelling either leads to withdrawal from participation in the public sphere or a rebellious attitude expressed through street violence or profound religiosity and camaraderie with orthodox practitioners.

I would like to raise some of Ghassan Hage's questions (2009: 257) in the context of the Cronulla riots and young Australian Muslims. He questions monoculturalism and multi-culturalism by stating that, "The monocultural assimilationists are never interested in the assimilation of the Other; they are interested in the process whereby they are trying to make them assimilate". He also questions whether such youth behaviour is a reaction against monoculturalism and whether there are fears that "they were completely assimilated and integrated despite their cultural differences" yet they did not have any politicised demands or program, just the will to hurt" (Hage 2009: 258, 260). Australian Muslim youth should be seen through the same lens as all youth groups and then it can be determined whether there is a difference due to religion or religious practice or whether they are behaving and doing what all young people are doing in Australia.

Conclusion

It has to be acknowledged that there are internal tensions in Muslim communities regarding the role of religion in life, identity and the nationhood project. The ongoing tension between moderates and conservatives within Islam is a concern for Australian Muslim communities and there are struggles not merely for dealing with *jihadist* mindset but for the rights of all Muslims. Declaring the veil as a signifier of religiosity and thus supporting terrorism or as being a statement against the "West" can potentially push more young women to adopt this form of dress code as a political statement and a mark of solidarity. This will further limit the possibility of any internal push for reform of women's rights within Islam, changing the dynamics and thus making younger Muslims inward looking and seeking solidarity within marginalised groups.

Muslim communities' need for schools and community centres in areas not highly populated by Muslims is a continuing cause of concern yet at the same time ghettoes of Muslim communities are criticised and even detested for failing to assimilate and integrate into mainstream society. How can these communities be expected to assimilate and integrate by simultaneously being refused entry into nationhood, labelled the "Other" and assigned a segregated public space for community life?

Muslim communities need to understand that in liberal democracies freedom of expression and diversity in views about religion or religious practices are fundamental rights and Muslims enjoy these rights like all Australian citizens. Faith, religion and religious rituals and practices will be viewed differently or criticised in ways that might seem insensitive or even hurtful, yet the diversity of views has to be accepted. Similarly it has to be recognised by mainstream society that one cannot claim freedom of expression for oneself and demand the banning of the veil through legislative measures at the same time. Western liberal democracies are founded on the principles of separation of state and religion. Demands for state intervention to deal with one faith group can potentially blur these boundaries and increase the outreach of the state in the private sphere.

Current socio-cultural anxieties need to be constructively addressed rather than dismissed. Muslim communities need to understand the anxieties and the fear of the unknown by mainstream communities and seek agency through legitimate participation in the nationhood project and be vocal in rejecting acts of violence in the name of religion. Mainstream society needs to understand that Muslim communities have similar concerns regarding terrorism, and that denial of agency silences the rational voices. A greater understanding of various pieces of legislation would help all communities to better understand their responsibilities and the inclusion of all Australian communities through engagement would address issues of engagement and restore fractured social relationships among Australian communities.

References

Albinski, Henry S. 2002. Australia, the terrorism phenomenon and the United States. *AQ: Australian Quarterly* 74 (2): 15–20, 40.

Bendle, Mervyn F. 2008. *Hijacking terrorism studies*, www.quadrant.org.au/magazine/issue/2008/9/hijacking-terrorism-studies (accessed 4 September 2010).

Bergin, Anthony, David Martin and Carl Ungerer. 2007. Beyond belief: Islamism, radicalisation and the counter-terrorism response. *Strategic Insights* 37, www.aspi.org.au/publications/publication_details.aspx?ContentID=140 (accessed 4 September 2010).

Bhatia, Michael V. 2005. Fighting words: Naming terrorists, bandits, rebels and other violent actors. *Third World Quarterly* 26 (1): 5–22.

Bleich, Erik. 2009. Where do Muslims stand on ethno-racial hierarchies in Britain and France? Evidence from public opinion surveys, 1988–2008. *Patterns of Prejudice* 43 (3): 379–400.

Carragee, Kevin M. and Wim Roefs. 2004. The neglect of power in recent framing research. *Journal of Communication* June 2004: 214–233.

Chesney, Robert. 2003. Civil liberties and the terrorism prevention paradigm: The guilt by association critique. *Michigan Law Review* 101: 1408–1452, http://works.bepress.com/robert_chesney/6 (accessed 4 September 2010).

Crewe, Emma and Priyanthi Fernando. 2006. The elephant in the room: Racism in representations, relationships and rituals. *Progress in Development Studies* 6: 40.

Duffield, Mark. 2006. Racism, migration and development: The foundations of planetary order. *Progress in Development Studies* 6: 68.

Hage, Ghassan. 2009. "Zionists" in lines in the sand. In *The Cronulla riots, multiculturalism and national belonging*, ed. Greg Nobel. Sydney: Institute of Criminology.

Hancock, Nathan. 2002. *Terrorism and the law in Australia: Legislation, commentary and constraints*, Research Paper No. 12, 2001–2002. Law and Bills Digest Group, 19 March 2002, www.aph.gov.au/library/pubs/rp/2001–02/02rp12.htm (accessed 4 September 2010).

Jackson, Richard. 2005. *Writing the war on terrorism: Language, politics and counter-terrorism.* Manchester: Manchester University Press.

Kerbaj, R. 2007. Fear keeps Muslims silent on terrorism. *The Australian*, 28 May 2007, www.theaustralian.com.au/news/nation/fear-keeps-muslims-silent-on-terrorism/story-e6frg6nf–1111113624217 (accessed 4 September 2010).

Kothari, Uma. 2006. An agenda for thinking about "race" in development. *Progress in Development Studies* 6: 9.

Luck, Les. 2004. *The Australian perception of the threat and appropriate responses*, www.dfat.gov.au/media/speeches/department/041028_terrorism _responses.html (accessed 4 September 2010).

Malik, Maleiha. 2009. Anti-Muslim prejudice in the West, past and present: An introduction. *Patterns of Prejudice* 43 (3): 207–212.

Matar, Nabil. 2009. Britons and Muslims in the early modern period: From prejudice to (a theory of) toleration. *Patterns of Prejudice* 43 (3): 213–231.

McKinnon, Gabrielle. 2010. *Social cohesion and human rights: Would a Bill of Rights enhance social cohesion in Australia?* acthra.anu.edu.au/articles/McKinnon%20social%20cohesion.pdf (accessed 4 September 2010).

Meer, Nasar and Tariq Modood. 2009. Refutations of racism in the "Muslim question". *Patterns of Prejudice* 43 (3): 335–354.

Michael, Michális S. 2009. Australia's handling of tensions between Islam and the West under the Howard Government. *Asian Journal of Political Science* 17 (1): 45–70.
Moncrieffe, Joy M. 2006. *Beyond categories: Power, recognition and the conditions for equality*. Background Paper for the World Development Report. London: Overseas Development Institute.
Moncrieffe, Joy M. and Rosalind Eyben. 2007. *The power of labelling: How people are categorized and why it matters*. London: Earthscan.
Pickering, Sharone, David Wright-Neville, Jude McCulloch and Pete Lentini. 2007. *Counter-terrorism policing and culturally diverse communities*, www.arts.monash.edu.au/criminology/news.../counterterrorreport-07.pdf (accessed 4 September 2010).
Pollak, Richard. 2006. The rumble down under. *The Nation* January 9/16, 2006.
Polya, Gideon. 2005. *Australian anti-terror laws target Muslims, media and free speech*, www.countercurrents.org/aus-polya151105.htm (accessed 21 September 2010).
—. 2005. *Scholars threatened by Australian anti-terror laws*, www.countercurrents.org/aus-polya241105.htm (accessed 21 September 2010).
Pugliese, Joseph. 2006. Asymmetries of terror: Visual regimes of racial profiling and the shooting of Jean Charles de Menezes in the context of the war in Iraq. *Borderlands E-journal* 5 (1), www.borderlands.net.au/vol5no1_2006/pugliese.htm (accessed 21 September 2010).
Purdy, Margaret. 2005. Countering terrorism: The missing pillar. *International Journal* 60 (1): 3–24.
Roy, Edmond. 2005. *Police worried about legal action from anti-terrorism laws*, 27 September 2005, www.abc.net.au/ am/content/2005/s1469047.htm.
Sandler, Todd, John T. Tschirhart and Jon Cauley. 1983. A theoretical analysis of transnational terrorism. *The American Political Science Review* 77 (1): 36–54.
Smiles, Sarah. 2007. ALP hits out over attitudes to Muslims. *The Age*, 5 October 2007, www.theage.com.au/news/national/alp-hits-out-over-attitudes-to-muslims/2007/10/04/1191091281223.html (accessed 4 September 2010).
Spalek, Basia and Alia Imtoual. 2007. Muslim communities and counter-terror responses: "Hard" approaches to community engagement in the UK and Australia. *Journal of Muslim Minority Affairs* 27 (2): 185–202.

Veit, Raphael. 2005. Australia and counter-terrorism. *AQ: Australian Quarterly* 77 (5): 33–37, 40.

Vincent, Andrew. 2001. The war against terrorism and multiculturalism: Australia's first war of the new millennium. *Australian Quarterly* 73 (6): 8–10.

Young, Iris Marion. 2003. Inclusion and democracy. *Oxford Scholarship Online,* November 2003 (accessed 4 September 2010).

Reports

Australia deliberates: Muslims and non-Muslims in Australia, 2007, www.ida.org.au/content.php?p=dpprelease (accessed 4 September 2010).

Australian Government response to PJCIS review of security and counter-terrorism legislation, December 2008, www.ag.gov.au/www/agd/agd.nsf/Page/Publications_AustralianGovernmentresponsetoPJCISReviewofSecurityandCounter-TerrorismLegislation-December2008 (accessed 4 September 2010).

Backgrounder: Security environment update, 2004–2005, www.ag.gov.au/www/agd/agd.nsf/Page/Publications_Budgets_Budget2004_InformationSheets_Backgrounder-Securityenvironmentupdate (accessed 4 September 2010).

Counter-terrorism White Paper: Securing Australia: Protecting our community, Commonwealth of Australia, 2010, www.dpmc.gov.au/publications/counter_terrorism/index.cfm (accessed 4 September 2010).

Practitioners' guide to the national security information (criminal and civil proceedings), ACT 2004, www.ag.gov.au/www/agd/agd.nsf/Page/Publications_PractitionersGuidetotheNationalSecurityInformation%28CriminalandCivilProceedings%29ACT2004 (accessed 4 September 2010).

Terrorism law, www.aph.gov.au/library/intguide/law/terrorism.htm (accessed 4 September 2010).

Transnational terrorism: The threat to Australia, Commonwealth of Australia, 2004, www.dfat.gov.au/publications/terrorism/ (accessed 4 September 2010).

Websites

www.khilafah.com/index.php/analysis/asia/9014-australia-counter-terrorism-white-paper-directly-targets-islam-and-muslims (accessed 4 September 2010).

On the attack: Ben Haywood analyses Australia's anti-terrorism laws. *The Age,* 3 October 2005, www.theage.com.au/news/education-news/on-the-attack/2005/09/30/1127804655990.html?from=moreStories (accessed 4 September 2010).

www.islammonitor.org/ (accessed 4 September 2010).

www.aph.gov.au/House/committee/pjcis/securityleg/report/chapter3.pdf.

Learning from one another: Bringing Muslim perspectives into Australian schools, www.education.tas.gov.au/infostream/general2010/june/17jun/professional/learning-from-one-another-bringing-muslim-perspectives-into-australian-schools?SQ_DESIGN_NAME=printer_friendly (accessed 21 September 2010).

CHAPTER SIX

WAR ON TERROR AND SOCIAL COHESION: NATIONAL SECURITY DISCOURSE, SOCIAL IDENTITY AND COMMUNITY ORDER

ROBIN CAMERON

What is the "War on Terror"?

What may seem a simple question at face value requires some reflection. What exactly do we mean when we speak of the war on terror? It encompasses the post-September 11, 2001, interventions in Afghanistan and Iraq (see Sahin, Chapter 4). It has given rise to international cooperation on intelligence matters and international finance that may be used to support terrorism (see Feaver, Chapter 2). It includes a ranges of new laws enacted within states, generally expanded police surveillance and search powers (see, for example, Babacan, Chapter 3), and major regulations on certain public spaces such as airports and other high-flow transport hubs. So while the war on terror can be categorised as, on one hand, international interventions and, on the other, counterterrorism, it should not be seen as necessarily synonymous with either. For instance, as many critics have suggested, the war on terror has *not* resulted in efficacious international interventions. The invasion of Iraq has been widely condemned and the achievability of the stated goals in Afghanistan has also been disputed. Similarly in a domestic context, many critics would suggest that the war on terror is *not* manifested as effective counter terrorism. Critics further suggest that effective interventions and counter terrorism policy are more likely to occur under policies and rubrics that are less divisive than the current policies of the war on terror. In this sense, there is a broader rhetoric and mindset that can also be attributed as a key characteristic of the war on terror.

What then, is this broader notion of the war on terror and what does it mean in the context of social cohesion? The war on terror is not limited to the formal counter-terrorism policies carried out by authorities. It is a global discourse that operates at the level of the politics between nation-states, at the party-political levels within nation-states and between and within local communities.[1] The war on terror is a social and cultural phenomenon interpreted, perceived and acted upon differently by various social groups within society other than those actively involved with counter terrorism. Different social groups, indeed different individuals, receive and internalise the ideas and norms that are implicit and explicit within the war on terror. This means that the war on terror can manifest independently of formal counter-terrorism measures in wider social contexts, as will be shown in the case of the Cronulla riots. The war on terror feeds into existing processes of social regulation, at which point formal policy positions take on a life of their own. Thus counter terrorism and its association with the war on terror is not limited to direct applications of the law but interacts with the complex web of social interactions that occur with reference to this political paradigm of the war on terror. It is in this manner that this chapter suggests that counter terrorism and the war on terror impact upon social cohesion.

This chapter suggests that it is important to "decouple" the war on terror and counter terrorism. As already suggested, it is not sufficient to regard the war on terror as simply policy responses to the events of September 11, 2001. There is a broader mindset at play, which significantly influences social cohesion. There are three instances in which counter terrorism and the war on terror have been used interchangeably. In the first instance, the post-September-11 rhetoric of a "war on terror" at home and abroad, purveyed most notably by US President George W. Bush, but adopted widely by many other national leaders, has defined the security priorities in the post-September-11 epoch. These priorities include war in Afghanistan, cooperation between national intelligence agencies and police forces, and a massive intensification of counter terrorism and surveillance at home. In this sense, counter terrorism has come to be seen as a key element of the war on terror. Secondly, among those critical of the post-September-11 security practices at home and abroad, the language of the war on terror has equally proliferated. Within academia and critical journalistic commentary, the terminology of war on terror has been used to refer to a wide range of practices from large-scale overseas wars and rendition for the purposes of torture to more stringent screening at airports and calls for greater community vigilance in local neighbourhoods. Again,

[1] For a detailed account of the nature of the war on terror discourse, see Jackson, Richard. 2005. *Writing the war on terrorism: Language, politics and counterterrorism*. Manchester: Manchester University Press.

counter terrorism is unavoidably associated with the war on terror. The potent rhetorical labelling of a new epoch of security concerns, combined with a tendency to criticise equally and simultaneously counter terrorism and the war on terror, has meant that counter terrorism, in whatever form it may take, has become associated by the wider public with the broad principles and wider discourse of the war on terror as it has been articulated at a global level and domestically by governments. In this sense, the war on terror is a broad social and political paradigm, one that even as it is contested at a global or national political level will continue to have lingering effects within communities.

Global War on Terror as a Paradigm of International Politics

The opening discussion has suggested an interpretation of the war on terror that is not solely limited to direct counter-terrorism measures. It suggests that there is more to the war on terror than its articulation as a global war. What is the war on terror in this broader sense? A crucial dimension of the global war on terror (and this will be equally evident in domestic manifestations) is the distinction drawn between friends and enemies, a tendency towards the use of language that portrays the world as a dualistic or Manichean arena of those who support the US and those who in stark contrast would wish it harm. This is expressed literally and paradigmatically in the language of US President George W. Bush. The infamous statement that "you're with us or you're with the terrorists" may have been rendered almost banal by repetition but the underlying logic has become very pervasive.[2] The friend-enemy distinction can also be seen in a number of more subtle ways in international discourse. For instance, in relation to which states can be considered civilised and what it means to be "civilised", a set of assumptions pervades discourses and policies of development and democracy promotion.

The operation of the friend-enemy distinction in the politics of national security was explored in the work of German legal theorist Carl Schmitt. Schmitt advocated what could be described as a radical variant of

[2] Bush, George W. 2001. *Address to a joint session of Congress and the American people, 20/09/01*. White House: President George W. Bush. georgewbush-whitehouse.archives.gov/news/releases/2001/09/20010920-8.html (accessed 22 August 2009).
See also Rothe, Dawn and Stephen L. Muzzatti. 2004. Enemies everywhere: Terrorism, moral panic, and US civil society. *Critical Criminology* 12 (3): 327–350.

realpolitik. Under this conception, not only would the national interest of the state be placed above that of other states but also above its own liberal democracy. Such a position arose out of Schmitt's critique of liberalism, which he felt was unable to address the harsh realities of politics, suggesting that it has "attempted to transform the enemy from the viewpoint of economics into a competitor and from an intellectual viewpoint into a debating adversary".[3] Schmitt's withering disdain for the weak-willed politics of liberalism captures the way in which calls for a more aggressive and assertive global role for the United States in the face of an emergent terrorist security threat were able to prevail over progressive voices in the post-September-11 political landscape. In the face of the threat of terrorism, the friend-enemy distinction became a potent force within international politics, whether for relations between nation-states or relations within Western democratic states. As Schmitt suggests, "every concrete antagonism becomes that much more political the closer it approaches the most extreme point, that of the friend-enemy grouping".[4] Other concerns, whether they be economic, legal, intellectual or ethical, become subsumed by expressly political demands as the distinction between friend and enemy grows more stark.[5]

The divisive language of the global war on terror has been ineffective when manifested as policy given the highly fluid nature of terrorism. Terrorist groups are not formalised bureaucracies with fixed bases in specific places. They are highly fluid, very adaptable and at times informal networks of people across national borders. A language that seeks to define fixed territorial entities as either seeking to prevent or alternatively supporting terrorism fails to grasp the extent to which such networks are interwoven throughout many different states, including Western states that offered a high degree of support for US actions in Afghanistan. Furthermore, this friend-enemy distinction can create false associations between terrorism and nation-states that, for whatever reason, are not among those considered part of an alliance of civilised states. In particular, the anti-Islamic sentiment implicit in the logic of the war on terror creates false associations between nation-states in the Middle East region and propensities towards an expectation of terrorism and radical interpretations of Islam. For example, among the many justifications for the invasion of Iraq were what turned out to be false associations with global terrorism; Iraq was a repressive secular state with antipathies towards religious

[3] Schmitt, C. 1976 [1934].*The concept of the political,* p. 28. New Brunswick, New Jersey: Rutgers University Press.
[4] ibid., p. 27.
[5] ibid., p. 37.

groups within its borders. The language of friend and enemy created an association between the Arab world and terrorism, a dualistic interpretive modality that carries through into domestic social relations.

The fluid nature of contemporary politics challenges the established distinctions between inside and outside. As Shapiro suggests, "the current security and intelligence policies dissolve many of the former distinctions between domestic crime-fighting and global warfare".[6] The inability to secure effective post-conflict peace in Afghanistan and Iraq has given cause for many to question the effectiveness of conventional war-fighting tactics in the war on terror. It has also resulted in the emergence of a greater focus on policing and order abroad. The Iraq war in particular has raised a much wider level of dissent within US politics over the motivations behind the decision to go to war and the appropriateness of the invasion in effectively countering terrorism. The extra-legal detention and abuse of prisoners held at the US-controlled Abu Ghraib and Guantanamo Bay detention facilities have received wide condemnation. Within domestic politics there has been fierce debate in the media and between political pundits over the balance between security and civil liberties and the appropriateness of torture as a tool of interrogation. The Bush Administration passed legislation – whose legality was supported by sympathetic intellectuals – that facilitated greater presidential powers. At the other end of the spectrum, citizens were also called upon to act according national security prerogatives.

These exceptional measures have been accompanied by an intensification of less overt mechanisms of control that are equally justified according to principles of national security. For instance, surveillance – albeit for the most part passive – has moved into many aspects of our day-to-day lives. Indeed, most of our technologically assisted communications and interactions with the world in advanced technological societies are now surveilled. Within the US surveillance has become widespread and immersive; telephone records, telephone conversations, internet usage, electronic funds transfers, cash withdrawals, overall consumption and spending patterns, even library borrowing records, are all either passively surveilled or able to be checked. As data-mining become more extensively employed, this surveillance will become largely passive but will nonetheless be constant. Similar systems are employed throughout most developed states. In the immediate proximity of strategic sites – a transport hub, a government or corporate building, a state monument or any populated public area – surveillance is carried out to counter possible

[6] Shapiro, Michael. 2005. Every move you make: Bodies, surveillance and the media. *Social Text* 83 23 (2): 27.

threats, whether general or specifically related to terrorism. Thus, in many densely populated areas bodies move within space that is highly controlled by processes of passive or active surveillance. While terrorism is not the sole risk that this pervasive surveillance seeks to counter, it is the predominant threat paradigm against which such measures are seen as necessary and are accordingly justified.

The emergence of direct regulation and pervasive surveillance cannot occur in a discursive or contextual vacuum. The adoption of wider executive or wartime powers is not only the result of particular extraordinary events but also of processes through which the political space throughout the Western political landscape has become securitised. September 11 has given rise to an exceptional state of politics, even though this is not the result of a formal suspension of the law or an out-and-out declared state of emergency. The response to the threat of terrorism has imbued politics with a general tenor of national security, which has derived a measure of support for practices that would otherwise be unacceptable in Western democracies. Divergent perspectives within Western nations have ensured that these developments have been far from uncontested and that there has been much resistance. This, however, has not stopped the emergence of these measures, which, given the tenor of the national security discourse, take a significant amount of courage and fortitude to resist. This was particularly the case in the initial years following September 11 when resistance would have been construed as equation with the nation's enemies – a clear demonstration of the operation of the regulatory power of the war on terror discourse upon domestic citizens.

The rise of an aggressive interventionism abroad and an emergency mentality at home following September 11 is furthermore suggestive of a politics of exception in the manner described by Carl Schmitt. This can be seen in the potent reassertions of sovereign authority during the Bush Administration, particularly in regard to the extension of executive presidential wartime powers. Schmitt defined sovereignty not in legal terms but in terms of the ability to act and the ability to decide, especially in times of emergency. According the Schmitt, the "sovereign is he who decides upon the exception".[7] The Bush Administration drafted legal opinions conferring wide-ranging wartime presidential powers, including the potential for the military to be employed domestically against terror suspects.[8] The drafting of those memos authorising greater domestic

[7] Schmitt, Carl. 1984. *Political theology: Four chapters on the concept of sovereignty*, p. 5. Cambridge, Massachusetts: MIT Press.

[8] Lewis, Neil A. 2009. Bush administration memos claimed vast war powers. *New*

power and willingness to act unilaterally abroad was an attempt by the Bush Administration to act decisively in the face of the September 11 attacks, demonstrating it would not be held hostage to acts of terrorism or wait for the tide of public opinion to determine its course of action. Such actions, understood in Schmittian terms, were an attempt to reassert the coherence of the state in the face of actions that undermined its authority. The integrity of the state became paramount, elevated above established practices of international law and normal rules and procedures – indeed some constitutional – designed to protect domestic liberty.

The exceptional politics of Schmitt is captured by the literature on securitisation, emerging largely from the Copenhagen School. This school of thought seeks to add a further theoretical dimension to security studies, drawing on the constructivist approach within International Relations.[9] In securitisation theory, security is not understood as an objective process but as the outcome of a process whereby notions of security are socially constructed by what these authors describe as "speech acts", essentially a narrowly defined notion of discourse. Ole Wæver, a key proponent of securitisation theory, suggests that "it is by labelling something a security issue that it becomes one".[10] Securitisation theory can thus be understood as "the intersubjective establishment of an existential threat with a saliency sufficient to have substantial political effects".[11] While Schmitt did not employ explicitly constructivist terms, securitisation theory "mirrors the intense condition of existential division, of friendship and enmity that constitutes Schmitt's concept of the political", so as to consolidate the state in order to face the threat.[12] Michael C. Williams expands the scope of securitisation, suggesting that the identification of enemies and the

---

York Times, 03/03/09 www.nytimes.com/2009/03/03/world/americas/03iht-terror.1.20553923.html (accessed 22 August 2009);

Savage, David G. 2009. Bush administration memos on presidential powers stun legal experts. *LA Times*, 04/03/09 articles.latimes.com/2009/mar/04/nation/na-bush-memos4 (accessed 22 August 2009).

[9] For the key thinkers and key text in this school of thought, see Buzan, Barry, Ole Wæver and Jaape de Wilde. 1998. *Security: A new framework for analysis*. Boulder, Colorado: Lynne Rienner.

[10] Quoted in Taureck, Rita. 2006. Securitization theory and security studies. *Journal of International Relations and Development* 9 (1): 54.

[11] Lausten, Carsten Bagge and Ole Wæver. 2003. In Defence of religion: Sacred referent objects for securitization. *Millennium Journal of International Studies* 29 (3): 708.

[12] Williams. Michael C. Words, images, enemies: Securitization and international politics. *International Studies Quarterly* 47 (4): 516.

construction of threats are not limited to words or "speech acts".[13] Williams instead locates securitisation within "a broader vision of communicative action", in which images and iconography play an equally important role.[14] Drawing on Williams' definitions, it can be suggested that securitisation involves a wider range of discursive processes than speech *per se* or, for that matter, images. Security concerns are thus intimately bound to the creation of identity and domestic processes of regulation and social cohesion.[15]

Domestic Manifestations of the War on Terror

What this chapter seeks to do, having articulated the nature of the global war on terror, is to link it to domestic order and social cohesion. The argument is that the war on terror is not only manifested domestically as counter terrorism but that it also operates independently as a discourse that shapes norms and social stereotypes, which counter terrorism in turn may also further consolidate. What links global phenomena like the war on terror to domestic social and cultural processes is, at the explicit level, the direct connection of global threats to domestic issues or, at a more subtle and often unintended level, the use of such discourses to frame domestic or regional concerns. The war on terror was a potent discourse that was readily evident following September 11 and could be readily observed in many key policy statements.

The Australian Government at an international level was one of the most vigorous supporters of the US in the war on terror. Australian Prime Minister John Howard provided rhetorical support and moral and legal justification of the war on terror as it was being carried out both at home and abroad. Howard prominently stated that "Australia will provide *all* the support that might be requested of us by the US in relation to *any* action that might be taken". [16] Indeed, Australia's soldiers were among the first to be deployed to Afghanistan and Iraq. Australia has thus been very much part of the global war on terror. Australia's strong support for the US in Afghanistan, Iraq and its regional interventions occasioned President Bush to comment that "the US sees Australia as a 'sheriff' of the Asia-Pacific". [17] Following this statement it became common to witheringly suggest that

---

[13] ibid., pp. 511–531.

[14] ibid., p. 524.

[15] See in particular Campbell, *Writing security*.

[16] Quoted in Harries, Owen. 2004. Don't get too close to the US. *The Australian*, 17/02/04.

[17] Quoted in O'Connor, Brendon. 2003. Perspectives on Australian foreign policy,

Australian foreign policy and in particular John Howard viewed himself as a "deputy sheriff". Statements such this and the "with us or against us" commonly attributed to Bush are, first of all, not correct quotations and, secondly and more importantly, tend to generalise and simplify national policy positions into trenchant statements. This, for all its reductionism, is the frame through which much of Australia is likely to understand the rhetoric of Australia's role in this global conflict – as a deputy sheriff in the war on terror.

The Bali bombings of 2002 brought the war on terror home on a more visceral – and less rhetorical – level as an immediate regional concern. This event brought the threat of terrorism to the direct attention of most Australians. Many Australians were injured in the bombings and Australia authorities were swiftly deployed to assist in the rescue and the investigation into the staging of the attacks. The sense of identification with Bali for many Australians was strong given that it is a popular holiday destination, familiar to many. Following these attacks the regional threat of terrorism was brought closer still to home by talk of an arc of crisis or arc of instability developing across the Pacific. Countries throughout the region were portrayed as emerging regional security threats, with their lack of development and modern forms of governance quickly correlated with the potential for terrorism to emerge from these societies.

The language of "failed states" was employed in particular to group these concerns. Prior to September 11 and the Bali bombings, Australian Foreign Minister Alexander Downer suggested that in the context of our region "a failed state is a state that could be exploited… by people like money launderers, drug traffickers, people traffickers and so on".[18] Following September 11 and the Bali bombings, this regional instability become increasingly connected with the discourse of the war on terror because of being framed in terms of reference to the war on terror. No longer was the main regional concern a lack of effective governance but rather sites for the emergence of terrorist threats against Australia. Indeed, a report by the Australia Strategic Policy Institute, widely cited by the media, suggested that the Solomon Islands "has to some extent already become… a Petri-dish in which transnational and non-state security threats

---

2003. *Australian Journal of International Affairs* 58: 214.

[18] Australian Foreign Affairs Minister, Alexander Downer. It is worth noting that in this interview he said it was "less likely that a failed state would be exploited by terrorists", which demonstrates the evolutionary nature of discourse. Taken from a media interview with Trisha Duffield, 2SM, Solomon Islands, 3/7/2001, http://www.dfat.gov.au/media/transcripts/2003/030701_solomons.html.

can develop and breed".[19] With the emergence of this more potent discourse of regional terrorism and the US policies of pre-emption and interventionism, Australia's decision not to be involved in regional interventions quickly dissipated as the war on terror became linked to regional security. John Howard announced: "We have sent a very large force to the Solomon Islands because it is in Australia's interest as well as the interests of all the people of that small country that it not become a failed state. Failed states become magnets for international criminals and money launderers and potentially international terrorists".[20] The regional intervention in the Solomon Islands was justified with reference to the discourse on the war on terror.

The war on terror embedded itself within a domestic context in a range of different ways. One highly influential means through which this occurred was the government's public information campaigns. Perhaps the most notable was the widely ridiculed fridge magnet, distributed to many Australian households as part of the "Be alert, not alarmed" public awareness campaign designed to increase awareness of, and resilience to, potential terrorists within Australia communities. This initiative became a highly visible articulation of the war on terror in the context of Australia for it not only operated as a fridge magnet distributed to many households but it also became highly recognisable as a point of ridicule within popular culture. It could be lampooned on comedy shows without the need for explanation of its context, suggesting a high level of awareness within society. This initiative was just one memorable part of a broad range of public awareness promotions. The "Be alert, not alarmed" campaign also ran a series of television advertisements that featured familiar Australian settings in which some detail was somewhat sinisterly not quite right. Breaks in chain-link fences near factories or garage lights on at late hours become signifiers for possible instances of terror threats in their planning stages. Vague enough not to be prescriptive, these advertisements encouraged the viewers to imagine familiar and personalised scenarios in which terrorism had a presence. The cultural diffusion of these public information awareness campaigns, while largely ineffective as a means of providing accurate information that would increase social cohesion, consolidated the war on terror discourse within a distinctly Australian social and political context.

---

[19] Australian Strategic Policy Institute. 2003. *Our failing neighbour: Australia and the future of Solomon Islands*, p. 13.

[20] Howard, John. 2003. *Address to WA Liberal Party State Conference*, 2/08/03, parlinfo.aph.gov.au/parlInfo/download/media/pressrel/X71A6/upload_binary/x71a66.pdf;fileType=application/pdf.

While not within the geography of Australia, the London bombings raised the spectre of "home-grown terrorism" for many Australians. The attacks upon the recognisable London Underground and iconic red buses presented a city, familiar and relatable to our own, subjected to major acts of terrorism. Furthermore, the United Kingdom, with a common political heritage and similar cultural cross-sections to Australia, provided a comparable broader social and political milieu from which home-grown terrorists might emerge. In particular, the possibility of alienated and disaffected members of a multicultural Western country committing acts of terrorism resonated with existing community fears stemming from multiculturalism, such as fears of ghetto-isation and loss of job opportunities, and general racism. These domestic issues of multicultural community relations became configured into fears of foreign threats in the context of community relations when interpreted with reference to the war on terror. These factors together meant that the attacks on the London tube and buses were events with which not only many Australians could identify but also provided further gravity to the threats associated with the war on terror.

The war on terror discourse also fed into other relations involving race and difference. The ability of John Howard to run a national security election campaign and win on the issue of immigration and border protection highlighted the potential in the post-September-11 political landscape for national security to divide communities and electorates. A key event was the rescue of the occupants of the stricken KM Palapa by the Norwegian freighter MV Tampa in August 2001. After the rescue Australia refused to allow the Tampa to dock in Australia – the nearest port – for fear of having to admit the refugees to camps. This triggered an overhaul of border control policies, which deployed the military in a border enforcement role. Operation Relex involved using all three branches of the Australian Defence Force to "detect, deter and return" Suspected Unlawful Non Citizens (SUNCs) aboard Suspected Illegal Entry Vehicles (SIEVs).[21]

Two further maritime border events occurred immediately prior to the late-2001 federal election. Most controversially, a boat known as SIEV 4 was intercepted on 6 October just north of Christmas Island by border protection authorities, at which point it sank. Despite a subsequent inquiry that suggested the contrary, a number of Howard Government ministers claimed that the children had been thrown overboard in an act of shocking inhumanity. Most tragically, a boat bound for Australia sank in Indonesian

[21] Chambers, Peter. 2010. The rising tide of border security. *Inside Story*, 28 July 2010, inside.org.au/the-rising-tide-of-border-security/ (accessed 28 October 2010).

waters, killing 353 passengers. This area, although in Indonesian waters, was part of the border protection surveillance area of the Australian authorities. A Senate Select Committee found that no responsibility among Australian authorities could be determined but it queried how such a major disaster could occur within the operational area of Australian authorities. The children overboard affair and the sinking of the SIEV X became events that allowed Howard to frame the election around national security issues, in particular border protection, described in the Border Protection Bill of 2001 as Australia's "sovereign right to determine who will enter and reside in Australia".[22] This framing of difference abroad coalescing into difference within is the mobilisation of the politics of the war on the terror discourse within the broader context of border control.

The emergence of border protection as a distinct security issue saw the blurring of a wide range of terms into a broad discourse of foreign threat. First, the legal category of "refugees" was displaced by that of "asylum seekers". The latter term removes the presumed right to protection by other countries, reflecting Australia's determination that protection and refugee status is not automatic but a decision to be made by the Federal Government. Similarly, the descriptions "boat people", "illegal immigrants", "asylum seekers" and "refugees" are increasingly used interchangeable in everyday media reporting and commentary. Even the term "migrants" began to take on a pejorative connotation. The generalised war on terror discourse legitimated the fear of difference and foreignness, which in this iteration was somewhat subtle. The war on terror discourse was also manifested in border security debates. This final step in the formulation of border protection, framed within the broader context of the war on terror discourse, explicitly linked immigration policy to the threat of terrorism. It was argued that terrorists might use illegal channels of immigration, in particular boats carrying "asylum seekers", to penetrate Australian borders and commit acts of terrorism in its cities. While ostensibly trying to identify the potential for illicit migration channels which could be exploited by terrorists, it fed into a broad discourse linking difference, specifically racial difference and in particular that of Middle-Eastern appearance, to the post-September-11 threat of terrorism.

---

[22] Quoted in Kleist, J. Olaf. 2009. Refugees between pasts and politics: Sovereignty and memory in the Tampa crisis. In *Does history matter? Making and debating citizenship, immigration and refugee policy in Australia and New Zealand*, eds Klaus Neumann and Gwenda Tavan, p. 52. Canberra, ACT: ANU E Press.

Case Study: Cronulla Riots

> Alan, it's not just a few Middle Eastern bastards at the weekend, it's thousands. Cronulla is a very long beach and it's been taken over by this scum. It's not a few causing trouble. It's all of them.
> (Alan Jones, Sydney radio host reading an email on air, 2005)23

On 11 December 2005 the southern Sydney beachside suburb of Cronulla was visited by an outburst of violence and a break-down in public order. The Australian public watched in surprised horror as latent tensions within Sydney's communities flared into open conflict that was widely described in the media as the "Cronulla riots". Two groups identified as "patriotic white Australians" from the southern beaches and "ethnic Lebanese Australians" from the western suburbs targeted one another, also drawing in bystanders who happened to bear any physical resemblance to either group. The violence was triggered by an assault on two lifesavers by a group of men of "Middle-Eastern appearance". It was argued that this violence was also a product of many months of sexually demeaning insults directed at young white women at beaches by groups of youths who were of "Middle-Eastern appearance". As a result, a mass demonstration of up to 5,000 people – mostly white males – gathered, brandishing Australian flags and chanting nationalist and racist slogans. The mob violently assaulted a number of individuals who in many cases were not even necessarily of "Middle-Eastern appearance" but were identifiably "non-white". In retaliation, convoys of cars from the western suburbs tried to enter Cronulla, forcing the police to set up road-blocks and check-points, effectively locking down many southern suburbs.

This was not a random outbreak of violence. It was a carefully staged cultural and media event that was given impetus by a range of stereotypes drawn from the wider discourse of the war on terror. In the first instance, there was widespread coordination of the event. Text messages encouraging people to take part in "Leb and wog bashing [sic]" were widely circulated within social groups living in and around the southern Sydney coast of the Cronulla Shire. These text messages were subsequently read out on public radio and published in Sydney and national newspapers under the pretext of reporting the emerging conflict. Whether intentional or naively lacking foresight, this publicity further

---

[23] Quoted in Marr, David. 2005. Alan Jones: I'm the person that's led this charge. *The Age*, 13/12/05, www.theage.com.au/articles/2005/12/12/1134236003153.html (accessed 9 October 2009).

inflamed the tensions.[24] Right-wing media personalities, in particular, built upon this emerging populist nationalistic sentiment by encouraging a "community show of force" to "reclaim" southern beachside suburbs.[25] The imagery involved in the lead-up to the violence was extremely potent. In Australia the image of the red-and-yellow-capped tanned lifesaver is a revered national symbol, almost iconographic in terms of its resonance. An assault on altruistic lifesavers is a symbolic assault on the collective national psyche. Similarly, the portrayal in the media of men of Middle-Eastern appearance making sexually demeaning comments to bikini-clad female beach-goers evoked the debates surrounding the repression of women's freedom within Muslim communities and the perceived chauvinism of societies in which women are perceived as being forced to wear burqas. Within a context of widespread media hype, such social imagery became highly provocative.

Beyond this, however, the wider international context of the war on terror played a vital role in precipitating social conflict. Since the September 11 attacks in New York and Washington, Australia had been subject to a range of measures designed to counter the threat of terrorism. These included, as discussed earlier, expanded police powers, increased surveillance, a range of social awareness campaigns and restrictions on immigration and the granting of asylum. This created throughout the Australian population a distinct image of a threatening terrorist Other of "Middle-Eastern appearance". Five months prior to the violence in Cronulla, the threat of terrorism had been brought closer to home by the London bombings of 7 July 2005. The reorientation of the threat from "terrorists abroad" to "home-grown terrorists" added a national security dimension to inter-community tensions that already existed between different areas of metropolitan Sydney.

The representation of the terrorist threat through this global discourse of the war on terror played a role in precipitating the break-down of order that occurred in Cronulla. Stereotypes of Anglo-Saxon patriotic nationalism and Islam as a threat to Western values that had been deployed

---

[24] Nguyen, Kenneth. 2007. Jones "incited" Cronulla violence on air. *The Age*, 11/04/07. www.theage.com.au/news/national/jones-incited-cronulla-violence-on-air/2007/04/10/1175971098057.html (accessed 9 October 2009);
See also Poynting, Scott. 2006. *Multiculturalism at the end of the line?* Paper presented at Everyday Multiculturalism Conference, Macquarie University, 28–29 September 2006, pp. 2-4. www.crsi.mq.edu.au/news_and_events/documents/scottpoynting_000.pdf (accessed 9 October 2009).

[25] Price, Steve, quoted in Poynting, Scott. 2006. What caused the Cronulla riot? *Race and Class* 48 (1): 86.

throughout the war on terror coalesced with the tense local issues described above to generate an outburst of public violence. A global discourse became entwined with domestic processes of identity and social cohesion. It reinforced social stereotypes and provided a rationale for public behaviour that some groups adhered to, some rejected, but all were aware of. In this sense, the global war on terror, the interventions it legitimised and the counter-terrorism measures it facilitated are no different from domestic policies and initiatives on matters such as policing or health that likewise engender social forces and inform cultural stereotypes, which shape and regulate social cohesion.

Identity and Belonging in the War on Terror

The significant element of the Cronulla riots is the complex politics and social relations connected to identity and belonging. For instance, should the two groups in question, those that identify themselves as ethnic Lebanese and those that identify themselves as patriotic white Australians, be regarded as groups which have an authentic sense of security and belonging, however negative the manifestations of this belonging may be? Or is it an inauthentic identity based solely upon a reactionary stance against another perceived identity group, which consolidates a false sense of belonging among individuals who otherwise may not share such a strong sense of cohesion? These stratified conceptions of identity and belonging should not be seen as fixed oppositions that require a choice of one or the other; rather they are social constructed stereotypes which, along with a range of other stereotypes, inform a complex and varied spectrum of identities. This is the fragile nature of securitised identities in the context of the war on terror. An existential or communal sense of security is informed by the stereotypes of the war on terror. The sense of security relies on one hand upon an equation of "Middle-Eastern appearance" with deviance and criminality so as to create cohesion among those who identify with stereotypes of Australian nationalism and patriotism. On the other hand, the sense of security relies on a sense of an oppressive elitist white majority that fails to recognise ethnic traditions in order to develop solidarity among those living in Sydney's western suburbs. Perceived racial differences are not simply markers of identities or fields of social cohesion but rather signify what is secure and what is threatening towards the nation. The war on terror has mobilised the discourse on national security into the relations of group identity and social cohesion.

The heightened tensions between racial identities and the lack of broad social cohesion across Sydney should not be seen as characteristics of "normal" politics. The global discourse of the war on terror operates as a particularly potent mechanism through which domestic identities are imbued with the dynamics designed to mediate difference at an international level. The stereotypes of the war on terror and those of patriotic Australian nationalism and Middle-Eastern radicalism can be seen as creating structural social impediments to effective negotiation of difference between identities and reducing the effectiveness of mechanisms around which social cohesion may be constructed. The operation of the war on terror discourse can be seen as facilitating a state of anomic relations between the particular racial identities in question. Anomie occurs when the mechanisms of social cohesion within communities are broken, resulting in crime and deviant behaviour. The Cronulla riots were outbreaks of what could be described as a misguided vigilantism against Middle-Eastern racial stereotypes who, within the context of the post-September-11 political landscape, were deemed threatening to the Australian way of life. In the opposing group there was a rebellious reconstruction and assertion of what are seen as Middle-Eastern ethnic traditions – still, however, within the context of Australian social relations – against Western modernity.

This chapter has suggested that counter terrorism should not be seen as synonymous with the war on terror. Indeed, upon decoupling these two terms and treating the war on terror as a field of discourse that legitimates repressive policies and facilitates a break-down in social cohesion, it would seem that the war on terror is in fact a major *impediment* to effective counter terrorism. Domestic counter-terrorism efforts not only have to address existing radicalism but must also attempt to de-securitise communities and identities that have become highly antagonistic as a result of their reorientation along the lines of war on terror stereotypes. Effective counter terrorism also needs to take into account the range of social and cultural effects of an unproductive national and global security discourse on a war on terror, which as we have seen, has created further radicalisation and loss of social cohesion within Australian communities such as the southern Sydney community of Cronulla. This study thus highlights the potency of national security discourse as an organising principle for everyday domestic social relations.

References

Australian Strategic Policy Institute. 2003. *Our failing neighbor: Australia and the future of Solomon Islands,* 10 June 2003, www.aspi.org.au/publications/publication_details.aspx?ContentID=30 (accessed 29 October 2010).

Bush, George W. 2001. *Address to a joint session of Congress and the American people*, 20 September 2001. White House: President George W. Bush, www.georgewbush-whitehouse.archives.gov/news/releases/2001/09/20010920-8.html (accessed 22 August 2009).

Buzan, Barry, Ole Wæver and Jaape de Wilde. 1998. *Security: A new framework for analysis.* Boulder, Colorado: Lynne Rienner.

Campbell, David. 1992. Writing security: United States foreign policy and the politics of identity. Minneapolis: University of Minnesota.

Chambers, Peter. 2010. The rising tide of border security. *Inside Story*, 28 July 2010, www. inside.org.au/the-rising-tide-of-border-security/ (accessed 28 October 2010).

Duffield, Trisha. 2001. *2SM, Solomon Islands*, 3 July 2001, www.dfat.gov.au/media/transcripts/2003/030701_solomons.html (accessed 10/8/11).

Harries, Owen. 2004. Don't get too close to the US. *The Australian*, 17 February 2004.

Howard, John. 2003. *Address to WA Liberal Party State Conference*, 2 August 2003, www.parlinfo.aph.gov.au/parlInfo/download/media/pressrel/X71A6/upload_binary/x71a66.pdf;fileType=application/pdf (accessed 10/8/11).

Jackson, Richard. 2005. *Writing the war on terrorism: Language, politics, counterterrorism.* Manchester: Manchester University Press.

Kleist, J. Olaf. 2009. Refugees between pasts and politics: Sovereignty, and memory in the Tampa crisis. In *Does history matter? Making and debating citizenship, immigration and refugee policy in Australia and New Zealand*, eds Klaus Neumann and Gwenda Tavan, 47–65. Canberra, ACT: ANU E Press.

Lausten, Carsten Bagge and Ole Wæver. 2000. In defence of religion: Sacred referent objects for securitization. *Millennium: Journal of International Studies* 29 (3): 705–739.

Lewis, Neil A. 2009. Bush administration memos claimed vast war powers. *New York Times*, 3 March 2009, www.nytimes.com/2009/03/03/world/americas/03iht–terror.1.20553923.html (accessed 22 September 2009).

Marr, David. 2005. Alan Jones: I'm the person that's led this charge. *The Age*, 13 December 2005, www.theage.com.au/articles/2005/12/12/1134236003153.html (accessed 9 October 2009).

Neumann, Klaus and Gwenda Tavan, eds. 2009. *Does history matter? Making and debating citizenship, immigration and refugee policy in Australia and New Zealand*. Canberra, ACT: ANU E Press.

Nguyen, Kenneth. 2007. Jones "incited" Cronulla violence on air. *The Age*, 11 April 2007. www.theage.com.au/news/national/jones-incited-cronulla-violence-on-air/2007/04/10/1175971098057.html (accessed 9 October 2009).

O'Connor, Brendon. 2004. Perspectives on Australian foreign policy, 2003. *Australian Journal of International Affairs* 58: 214.

Poynting, Scott. 2006a. *Multiculturalism at the end of the line?*, Everyday Multiculturalism Conference, Macquarie University, 28–29 September 2006, www.crsi.mq.edu.au/news_and_events/documents/scottpoynting_000.pdf (accessed 9 October 2009).

—. 2006b. What caused the Cronulla riot? *Race and Class* 48 (1): 85–94.

Rothe, Dawn and Stephen L. Muzzati. 2004. Enemies everywhere: Terrorism, moral panic and US civil society. *Critical Criminology* 12: 327–350.

Savage, David G. 2009. Bush administration memos on presidential powers stun legal experts. *LA Times*, 4 March 2009, www.articles.latimes.com/2009/mar/04/nation/na-bush-memos4 (accessed 22 August 2009).

Schmitt, Carl. 1984. Political theology: Four chapters on the concept of sovereignty. Cambridge, Massachusetts: MIT Press.

—. 1976. *The concept of the political*. New Brunswick, New Jersey: Rutgers University Press.

Shapiro, Michael J. 2005. Every move you make: Bodies, surveillance and the media. *Social Text* 23 (2): 21–34.

Taureck, Rita. 2006. Securitization theory and security studies. *Journal of International Relations and Development* 9 (1): 53–61.

Williams, Michael C. 2003. Words, images, enemies: Securitization and international politics. *International Studies Quarterly* 47 (4): 511–531.

CHAPTER SEVEN

CREATING BELONGING: SAFETY, RACISM AND SOCIAL COHESION

HURRIYET BABACAN

Introduction

In the last decade there has been much public debate about social inclusion and exclusion, multiculturalism and social cohesion. Nation-states have engaged with these debates, mainstreaming social inclusion by establishing social inclusion units as agencies of government agencies (Jeannotte 2000). The cornerstone of the democratic nation-state is the establishment of rights: political, social and civil. Membership in a nation-state denotes both civic belonging in the political community and cultural belonging in a national community (Castles and Davidson 2000). However, in ethnically and culturally diverse societies belonging and inclusion have not been unproblematic. Vasta (2007: 3) points out that a number of concerns have arisen in Western societies about identity, specifically ethnic or religious identities versus a perceived homogenous national identity.

The foundations of contemporary Western societies have been very influenced by Durkheim's thinking on social cohesion in the 19th century. Durkheim provided the first systematic theorisation of the role and function of social integration and social cohesion, arguing that modern societies need to be held by a social glue. He asked the the question: "what are the bonds that unite men with one another?" This question goes to the core of norms, values, social capital and trust in societies. Durkheim argued that solidarity is the glue that holds society together and at the basis of this is the need for homogeneity. He wrote: "Society can only exist if there exists among its members a sufficient degree of homogeneity" (Durkheim 1956: 70). Durkheim argued that where social cohesion exists, it "can be traced to certain conformity of each individual consciousness to a common type, which is none other than the psychological type of society" (cited in Giddens and Sutton 2010: 25). He later labelled it "solidarity by similarities".

Contemporary Australia is a multicultural country with approximately 22% of its citizens born overseas. A further 18% have at least one parent born overseas. So 43% of all Australians were born overseas or have at least one parent who was born overseas, and in recent years, people from around 185 different countries have made their home in Australia. The composition of Australia's population has changed dramatically during the past 200 years. It has gone from an almost total Aboriginal population to predominantly Anglo-Celtic by 1900 and then to its present mix of about 74% Anglo-Celtic, 19% other European and 4.5% Asian. Twenty-one percent of Australians speak a language other than English at home. Australia is a multi-religious society (ABS 2006; DIAC 2007). These statistics alone challenge the concept of solidarity by similarity and homogeneity. Cultural homogenisation does not work and there is a need to recognise that migrants bring their cultures and histories with them (Westwood and Phizacklea 2000). Over the last 40 years in Australia, progress has been made in rejecting the assimilation of immigrants in favour of respect for cultural diversity. And since September 11 we have witnessed a new era in multicultural politics in Australia and other Western nations.

Soroka et al. (2007: 561) identify two compelling challenges facing contemporary Western societies: (1) how to respect cultural differences, expand the room for minorities to express their distinctive cultures and construct new and more inclusive forms of citizenship, and (2) how to reinforce the bonds of a community that is diverse with the need to incorporate newcomers into the economic and social mainstream, to sustain a sense of mutual commitment and solidarity in times of need, and to build a national identity. Three key questions emerge from these challenges: Who are we? – related to shared values and norms. How do we live together? – related to engagement, participation and social integration. How do we build social capital? – related to trust and social networks.

These agendas are important in diverse societies, and the emphasis on them by government has shifted back and forward. In the first decade of this new century, the balance of the debate is shifting again. There is renewed concern about the social integration of immigrants and threats to social cohesion. At the same time, the rhetoric of social inclusion and exclusion persists.

This chapter focuses on belonging, inclusion, racism and social cohesion within Australia. It is argued that social inclusion initiatives have been implemented without regard to social exclusion based on ethnicity, religion and "race". Major events in recent Australian history that have been a cause for concern include racially-motivated violence against Muslim communities, the Cronulla riots, attacks on international students, the vilification of asylum seekers and refugees, and other acts of racism. It is argued in this paper that social exclusion in Australia is articulated without denouncing democratic principles and through transformation into more palatable concerns. Coded societal messages are perpetuated through public discourses on the war on terror, immigration, multiculturalism, refugees and citizenship. The chapter concludes with an exploration of a way forward – namely, through reclaiming critical multiculturalism, participation and engendering a sense of equal valued status.

Inclusion, Exclusion and Racism

Migration processes uproot people and transplant them to a new environment, a transition that at the best of times is not easy. Community attitudes greatly influence successful integration into Australian society (Jupp et al. 1991). Australian attitudes towards immigrants reflect confusion, anxiety, scepticism, ambivalence, lack of knowledge and modern racism (Babacan 2007).

Management of diversity continues to be a central issue for Australia in the context of the public opinion which negatively targets immigrants. The advent of "globalised terrorism" in the wake of September 11 has resulted in the adoption of protective measures both nationally and internationally. Discourses on fighting the war on terror have been conjoined with other issues such as border protection, ethnic crime and threats to "Australian culture" from immigration. A climate of concern over safety and security has been created which has been vehement against particular groups of people. The adoption of a "protective framework" has been accompanied by an erosion of the civil liberties, freedoms and human rights traditionally associated with Western democracies. Since the 1990s, immigration and asylum have become highly politicised. In particular, the Howard Government engaged in the politics of fear and curtailment of the social and citizenship rights of asylum seekers (Castles 2003: 20) by portraying them as "exploitative" people whose aim was to "abuse" industrialised nations. Public discourses initiated by the government continue to depict asylum seekers as people who "abuse" Australia's refugee determination process and "threaten" the Australian community. Although such constructions were and remain unsubstantiated, they suited the Howard Government's longer-term policy agenda. Pickering, tracing asylum seeker issues through two Australian newspapers (*The Brisbane*

Courier Mail and *The Sydney Morning Herald)* between January 1997 and December 1999, demonstrated that the terms "illegal entrants" and "queue jumpers" had been used widely in public debates and that this had led to the "criminalisation" of "unauthorised" arrivals (Pickering 2001).

The post-2000 period has seen the conjoining of asylum to security matters. Public discourses relating to terrorism have been strongly linked to the process of creating "the other" as the threat. This has created suspicion of those who are deemed to be different. The "Be alert, not alarmed" campaign reinforced the elements of *fear* and *risk* in neigbourhoods, communities and public spaces in unprecedented ways. After September 11, the war on terrorism became a major issue around the world and became enmeshed with immigration and asylum issues (Hugo 2002: 39). As a significant proportion of the boat people arriving in Australia were of Islamic backgrounds, this allowed a connection to be made between asylum seekers and terrorists in public discourse. This marked a shift in the way those from the "Middle East", "Muslims" or "Arabic" were represented as both a potential terrorist threat and a cultural threat to the Australian way of life.

The fear politics pursued by the government has had a massive impact on race relations in Australia (Poynting and Noble 2004). Through their "association" with people smugglers, asylum seekers and refugees were depicted as criminals (Shaw 2001). During the Tampa standoff, the government's labelling of asylum seekers as a "threat" or "common enemy" enabled it to powerfully and effectively draw upon nationalistic discourses (Dreher 2001; Van Acker and Hollander 2003). These negative discourses worked to de-legitimise asylum seekers, thereby ensuring that in the public arena they were not seen as "genuine" refugees who were "worthy" of Australia's compassion. A political and social climate emerged, "in which asylum seekers, migrants and refugees are demonised as undesirable, undeserving, and overwhelming" (Ouseley 2004: 9). These qualities were presented in opposition to the purported Australian qualities of fairness, honesty, mateship and civility (Clyne 2005).

Taylor (2002) argues that government policies have led to an environment in which the distinction between asylum seekers and terrorists and the distinction between security concerns and the obligations owed to asylum seekers have become blurred and enmeshed. The Human Rights and Equal Opportunity Commission (HREOC) documented the extent of the targeting of Arabs, Muslims and others in an extensive national consultation with Australian Muslims. *Isma-Listen (*HREOC 2004) found that the majority of Muslims consulted had experienced escalating prejudice because of their race or religion. They reported experiences that ranged from "offensive remarks about race or religion to physical violence" (HREOC 2004: 2).

On 11 December 2005 the television screens of the nation carried shocking visual footage of what has come to be known as the "Cronulla riots". These were images of a violent, drunken mob of some 5000 mainly "white" male Australians, most with beer can in hand and many draped with the Australian flag, verbally abusing, attacking and beating the few individuals of "Middle Eastern appearance" they could find nearby (Collins 2006). The popular media assisted in the mobilisation of this mob. For example, on the radio Alan Jones read out the message, "This Sunday, every Aussie in the Shire get down to North Cronulla to help support Leb and wog bashing day" (Collins 2006). Jones, one of the most prominent of the Sydney shock-jocks, also encouraged support for the rally with the words "Come to Cronulla this weekend to take revenge". Callers to his program recounted many instances when young "Aussie" women had been insulted by Muslims or men of Middle Eastern appearance (Collins 2006; Manning 2006). In commenting on the Cronulla riots, the Prime Minister denied that there was any racism underlying these events. Poynting et al. (2004) argue that Howard's refusal to acknowledge racism as a cause of the Cronulla riots ignored the obvious fact that racism played a central role in the incidents and that the state's refusal to act on this was a clear message from the state for "permission to hate" (Poynting et al. 2004).

The literature on social exclusion has focused on this concept as being exclusion from the labour market, economic exclusion (including poverty), exclusion based on social isolation, geographic or spatial exclusion and exclusion based on institutional processes and systems. (Young 1999). Most of the literature on social exclusion makes no mention of exclusion based on "culture", "ethnicity" and "racism". It is important to acknowledge that social exclusion can take place on the basis of "culture" and "race".

New forms of racism no longer rely on biological definitions of inferiority or superiority but on exclusions based on cultural considerations. Racism now is often not demonstrated by direct acts of hostility but rather by covert comments relating to moral character, alien cultural values and lifestyles (Pedersen et al. 2004; Fraser and Islam 2000). Racism is not only reflected in events such as the "race riots" in Cronulla in 2005 but includes ordinary "everyday" racisms which are silently experienced by individuals and communities (Babacan and Babacan 2006; Essed 1991).

Defining *racism* is a difficult task as it changes its forms and meanings in different historical contexts. Racism operates through relational, systemic and institutional practices that serve to devalue, exclude, oppress or exploit people. It is an act of power and a means of maintaining privilege, and racialised hierarchies of power characterise social structures (Back and Solomos 2000; Babacan et al. 2009). There is considerable evidence that racism leads to social exclusion on the basis of culture, language and ethnicity as well as perceptions of "race". Studies indicate that the life chances of "racialised" minorities are adversely affected (Hollinsworth 2006; Bonnet 2000). Dunn et al. (in a research project on racism in which one of the authors is also a principal researcher) in a large national study demonstrated that 78% of Australians believe humankind is made up of separate races, 41% believe that there are cultural groups that do not fit into Australian society, 85% believe there is racial prejudice in Australia although, paradoxically, 87% believe that it is a good thing for society to be made up of different cultures. The same study found anti-Asian sentiment (24%), anti-Aboriginal sentiment (28%), anti-Muslim sentiment (49%) and anti-Semitic sentiment (23.3%).

Contemporary discourses on racism suggest that there is an abhorrence of racism and that it is an offence to modern sensibilities. There is a growing literature, however, that articulates that "new racism" operates in subtle forms that are difficult to identify (Henry et al. 2000; Dunn et al. 2007; Babacan 2008). This literature explores how racism can be expressed without denouncing democratic principles by transforming it into "legitimate" and contemporary concerns. Social messages are perpetuated through coded public discourses on immigration, multiculturalism, refugees and citizenship. Such "codes" reflect the power to represent others, to negatively evaluate others and to make these representations and evaluations prevail in public domains. These are the key features of the new racism (van Dijk 2000; Babacan and Babacan 2006). Resort to fear politics has facilitated and promoted the new racism in Australia (Gopalkrishnan and Babacan 2007). Racism is powerful in its capacity to generate fear of "others", a phenomenon that is widely understood as being a powerful tool for governments and corporations to shape public discourse and behaviour (Gopalkrishnan 2007). If the government is constrained from providing anything more than minimal support to citizens, what do politicians draw on to attract voters? In a world based on neoliberalism, the use of fear has achieved a new level of sophistication and reach. The messages of fear become even more ominous when they are targeted on racial lines. Engaging in fear tactics enables a government to develop its vote bank and unite an in-group, and is a powerful instrument of rule (Gopalkrishnan 2007; Robin 2004). Fear of an external or internal foe can be more powerful than day-to-day issues of job insecurity, changing power relationships in the workplace, increasing indebtedness, loss of social support frameworks, alienation, and the sense of helplessness in the face of powerful forces. This fear impacts on people's ability to forge relationships and friendships in the community, with their neighbours, within school communities and at work. Research indicates that everyday racism continues in the streets, educational institutions and workplaces in Australia (Dunn et al. 2004; Babacan and Hollinsworth 2010).

Social Cohesion

The concept of *social cohesion* has entered the lexicon of Western governments and the loss of social cohesion is deplored (Jenson 2002; Babacan 2007). However, there is no agreement on what social cohesion is. The term is used broadly to encompass a large number of ideas, including social capital, social order, common aims and values, civic and political participation, trust, ethnic harmony, personal and national security and peace (Colenso 2005; Forrest and Kearns 2001). Jeannotte (2000) undertook a literature review and identified four important elements of social cohesion: it is a process rather than an end state; it requires social solidarity and determining who is "in" and who is "out" and to whom members of society owe solidarity; it is based on collective values and identity; and it relates to conflict resolution in pluralist societies. It is noted that the literature on the last element is not well developed and is mostly focused on social capital with insufficient attention to how conflict is resolved in democratic institutional frameworks. Also, while there is an abundance of literature on what threatens social cohesion, there is very little on what supports it (Jeannotte 2000). The factors that threaten social cohesion include: lack of citizenship; the "rights" model as a deficit; political disenchantment; economic disparities (unemployment, poverty, income inequalities); rural/regional disparities; urban distress; social exclusion; exclusion from the information society; retreat from intervention by the state; deterioration of the environment and quality of life; cultural diversity and demographic change; the influence of American global culture; changing values regarding work; and the shift to individualism (Jeannotte 2000: 13). Diversity, citizenship and social exclusion are seen to be linked with social cohesion, yet social exclusion literature, as noted above, skims over or ignores issues linked to cultural diversity. National identity and shared values feature strongly as factors which facilitate social cohesion (Jeannottee 2000; Jenson 2002; Babacan and Babacan 2006). Social cohesion literature focuses heavily on the threats from religious and cultural diversity. One fear is based on the premise that Western democratic values will be destroyed by too many foreigners or by immigrants whose values are perceived to be different or inferior. There is a perception among some that alleged different or inferior values may threaten national identity and have a damaging effect on social cohesion, leading to violence and to a loss of freedom. On the other hand, some contend that immigrants and ethnic minorities have not done what they were meant to do – that is, to become like "us". Many believe that immigrants have not met their responsibility to integrate, thus segregating themselves from the receiving society.

In Australia, the public discourse relating to social cohesion is linked to terrorism and diversity – the process of creating "the other" as "the threat". The manner in which the debates have been deliberately handled has led to the creation of suspicion of those who are deemed to be different. Discussion and debates have been interwoven with issues relating to Australian values and national identity and have ultimately reinforced particular types of patriotism. The current Australian Multicultural Policy states that it "responds to our cultural diversity and aims to strengthen social cohesion" (DIAC 2011: 2).

Today the stereotypical images of the stranger as asylum-seeker, migrant or refugee presented by the media and other networks often precedes the arrival of migrants. The war on terror has been accompanied by a grand narrative which has been interwoven with issues relating to Australian values and national identity and fear of the "other", and has reinforced particular types of patriotism. There have been deliberate attempts to create a unique and homogenous national identity that attempts to unite some parts of the community while excluding others (Babacan and Babacan 2006). This is a unilateral debate, driven mainly by the nation-state and aided by the media (Brett 2004). It involves the construction of Australian identity to reflect particular cultural groups and exclude others in the national interest. National identity is constructed as "a particular way of life, particular set of values represented by those who are white and of Anglo Saxon/Celtic backgrounds" (Dunn et al. 2004). McPherson (2010: 553) argues that the Australian Government saw cultural pluralism as posing "a threat, not just to the safety of Australians, but to the fabric or character of Australian society". The discourse on nationalism – of who is Australian and who is un-Australian – is telling. Attention to issues of character and values have been pronounced and attempts have been made to define Australian values, characteristics and way of life. "Un-Australian" draws lines of acceptability – delineating what is regarded as reasonable, proper and decent forms of public speech and behaviour. Who is an Australian, what are Australian values, who is the "Aussie battler" and what is "un-Australian" have been redefined and have had significant consequences for those who are included and excluded. Regular pronouncements by the Prime Minister, other ministers and media "license" such abuses while feeding feelings of dominance. Dominance is internalised in the dominant group and leads to the rejection of others (Dudgeon and Oxenham 1989). Powerful discourses invoke images of meritorious "Aussie battlers" – ordinary Australians who deserve respect and support. At the same time, as Carole Johnson observed, "ordinary Australians are not Aboriginal, Asian, homosexual, lesbian, feminist or migrant" (2000: 64-65). There has been a deliberate attempt to create a homogenous national identity that unites some parts of the community while excluding others. The new forms of patriotism that have emerged are racialised and draw boundaries of inclusion and exclusion. Research indicates that many ethnic minorities feel fearful and excluded (Dunn et al. 2004; Babacan and Hollinsworth 2010; Poynting and Noble 2004; HREOC 2004).

Kershan (2005) argues that there is a recurrence of key elements such as socio-economic disadvantage, media hostility, and the real or imagined anxiety that immigration is "out of control", which have been features of the politics of immigration over the last century. However, Kershan notes that what is now different is the combination of enduring and new variables, together with the changing global context of migration processes, and this change brings a sharp edge to the contemporary political saliency of immigration. With the advent of this form of racism, ethnic communities are differentiated as being a "threat to the cultural integrity" of the Anglo-Celtic host society (Dunn et al. 2004). Questions as to who does/does not belong to Australian society, what or who is/is not Australian are integral aspects of the intolerance to some groups and the new racism in Australia (Dunn et al. 2004). The answers to these questions have changed with time. The most recent examples include asylum seekers, Arabs and Muslims (Dunn et al. 2004). Essentially, the key element of *old racism*, the so-called "incompatibility" of different ethnic groups and their "inability" to co-exist, remains as an integral aspect of *new racism* (Corlett 2002). Overall there is a portrayal that the social fabric that links Australian communities is unravelling and so there is a need for tough government action against the threats. Babacan and Gopalkrishnan (2008) identify that these tough actions have focused on key areas. The attempt to maintain social cohesion has embarked on new forms of racism, both subtle and not so subtle , which are: Islamophobia, creating Muslim communities as the "other"; limited and differentiated citizenship rights; renewed attempts to create a national identity based on

Anglo-Saxon norms and the new wave of patriotism; and the permeation of everyday racism and "racism denial".

Solutions to the concern about the lack of social cohesion are presented in the form of a powerful political campaign which "emphasises a return through cultural renewal to a more secure – often mythical – idea of community" (Jayasuriya 2003: 3) and a return to the old times (Jenson 2002). There is an increasing concern about social solidarity, social order, and cohesiveness. The argument is that multiculturalism, immigration and asylum seekers are a threat to the social cohesion of Australian society. Similar arguments are seen in Europe, Canada and the USA. The reasons for these are linked with the paradigm shift towards neoliberalism, causing structural strains economically and politically (Babacan et al. 2009; Jenson 2002). Whether economic or political, the uncertainty and fear created is a threat to belonging and identity. The solution is seen in the abandonment of the last three decades of accepting multiculturalism in favour of what some call "a return to assimilation" (Cheong et al. 2005: 2) or assimilation in a new guise. The Australian Government response has been to develop an Australian Values Statement (DIAC 2010) which immigrants and refugees wishing to settle in Australia have to sign. This prescribes a set of values which immigrants must adopt and adhere to. However, this is a flawed approach. Social cohesion cannot be achieved without ethnic minorities developing a sense of belonging, both in terms of material inclusion and subjectively (Vasta 2007; Babacan and Babacan 2006). This cannot be engineered by the state (Amin 2002). The Values Statement and the Australian Citizenship Test both reflect the view of the immediate past and the present governments that a solution to social cohesion can be found in defining who it is "we" are in relation to "them" (McPherson 2010: 554).

Ways Forward

Immigrants in any context of migration want to be included in and belong to their host country without giving up their history, background and identity. Being socially included means:

- to participate as valued, appreciated equals in the social, economic, political and cultural life of the community;
- to be involved in mutually trusting, appreciative and respectful interpersonal relationships at the family, peer and community levels. (Crawford 2003: 5)

Jenson (2007) sets out the task ahead for social cohesion: the key dimensions are belonging versus isolation, inclusion versus exclusion, participation versus non-involvement, recognition versus rejection and legitimacy versus illegitimacy. There have been different approaches to tackling these challenges of creating a cohesive and inclusive society. The future is not about achieving homogeneity as Durkheim saw it but about finding ways to reconcile and appreciate our differences (Hall 1997). The Council of Europe has argued that the way forward comes with the need to expand the legal framework of human rights to include both social and cultural rights. In the face of "a disturbing rise in racism, anti-Semitism, xenophobia, ethnocentrism, religious fundamentalism and... intolerance and exclusion", the Council has devoted particular attention to cultural rights such as the rights to identity, language, heritage, education and participation in cultural life (Council of Europe 1997: 165). The Council makes the point that the challenge is in identity construction in modern Europe (and for that matter, in Australia) and the necessity of reconciling a series of multiple identities. However, until the notion of diversity is accepted and certain groups cease to be marginalised, the Council foresees continuing pressure on social cohesion (Council of Europe 2001). Thus, achieving social cohesion, among other political and economic factors, is through valuing cultural difference, fostering a sense of belonging, and the inclusion of those who are deemed the "other".

Bloch and Dreher (2009) remind us that immigrants consistently find that racism and harassment are predominantly experienced in public spaces. They see the challenge as being to find ways to engage the people who express these fears without encouraging and legitimising those fears (Block and Dreher 2009: 204). This approach is supported by Babacan's (2005) research in relation to built-up environments and "landscapes of fear". Wise (2006) focuses our attention on the importance of place and place sharing. She offers nuanced explorations of the practices and ethics of place-sharing in neighbourhoods and through neighbourly relations. Hage has termed this "a multiculturalism of inhabitance" (Hage 1998: 233). Zournazi and Hage point to our capabilities of sharing, trusting, building community, belonging and safety when they state that "we are capable of reaching even greater joyful leaps when we combine communally with others" (Zournazi and Hage 2002: 152). They describe "a sense of community as a sense of articulation to others… the feeling of connection, of sharing, or recognition" (Zournazi and Hage 2002: 162). This creates a feeling of homeliness which represents familiarity, community, security and hope (Zournazi and Hage 2002: 159–61).

Wise sums it up when she states:

> It is my argument that common to all these exchanges were certain forms of manners, recognition, gratitude and hospitality, which have the capacity to facilitate the development over time of forms of interethnic belonging, security and trust. Such interethnic social capital, as I term it, is an essential prerequisite for the creation of dispositions of the open, joyful and hopeful kind, full of possibilities for opening up to otherness. (Wise 2006: 182)

So while public debates call for a return to a nostalgic past, this form of community making is about closure and setting boundaries. As McPherson (2010: 546) notes, migration debates privilege conformance by "outsiders" as the path to social cohesion, and migrants and refugees are represented as problematic, deficient and in need of changing. Citizenship tests and language education classes are presented as the panacea, as vehicles for teaching "our values" and for rectifying problematic migrant subjectivities. What needs to happen is an opening to the other, to the different, and the development of mutual recognition and trust. Simmel's notion of "gratitude", of giving and receiving, makes it a powerful means of social cohesion (Simmel 1950), not through being thankful, but through its capacity to create innumerable connections, building bridges between strangers and expressing recognition and gratitude for one another's existence. This can only happen if the dominant discourses and norms, the "common sense" arguments about Australian and un-Australian, are interrupted.

According to Foucault, it is vital to draw upon "subjugated knowledges" of the marginalised as a way forward. Foucault (1980: 81–82) states that "subjugated knowledges" are:

> a whole set of knowledges that have been disqualified as inadequate to their task or insufficiently elaborated: naive knowledges, located low down on the hierarchy, beneath the required level of cognition or scientificity… It is through the reappearance of this knowledge, of these local popular knowledges, these disqualified knowledges… that criticism performs its work.

The creation of belonging, inclusion and cohesion in a diverse society comes from giving legitimacy to marginalised knowledges and lending a voice to the lived experiences of minorities. This entails abandoning the representations of ethnic minorities (through the media, state and corporations) as a deficit model or as problematic. The nation-state constructs multiculturalism and immigrants in particular ways in public discourse (Vasta 2007). The recent backlash and retreat from multicultural policy has weakened the support for diversity. Soutphommasane (2005) argues for a "civic pluralist model of multicultural citizenship" which must meet two tests: recognising cultural difference in the public sphere and providing a new basis for political belonging. This requires an "open" political culture or "deliberative democracy", in which political institutions and practices are exposed to scrutiny and re-interpretation, and a sense of belonging is based less upon shared political values and more upon common membership of public debate within a political community.

Hooghe (2007) reminds us of the importance of social capital and trust as fundamental elements for building social cohesion. He urges that in diverse societies, recognition of group differences and identities and group relations based on equality-based concepts of reciprocity should be considered as a potentially more meaningful strategy for recognition of cultural difference. The structures and processes of equality need to provide the basis and resources to expand multiculturalism. Vasta suggests four prerequisites for expanded multiculturalism: mutual accommodation – mutual recognition of core values, differences and repositioning of social cohesion; multiculturalism that embraces the whole society – not referring only to immigrants; equality and full participation; and racism – engaging with racism/racial discrimination as a fundamental social phenomenon deeply rooted in the histories, cultures, traditions and institutions of Western democracies (2007: 25–26).

The movement of people is a constant in a globalised world and ethnic heterogeneity is the norm. While nations deliberate about reconciling differences, it is apt to end the chapter with the words of caution from the Council of Europe (2001: 11):

> Acceptance of diversity and the interaction between cultures foster harmonious relations between people, enrich their lives and provide them with creativity to respond to new challenges. It is not the denial, but rather, the recognition of differences that keeps a community together. Without a respect for differences communities may turn in on themselves, ultimately leading to their disintegration, decline or disappearance. It may also lead to an identity lose and provoke aggression towards others.

References

ABS. 2006. *2006 Census quickstats*. Australian Bureau of Statistics, Canberra, www.censusdata.abs.gov.au/ABSNavigation/prenav/ViewData?subaction=-1&producttype=QuickStats&areacode=0&action=401&collection=Census&textversion=false&breadcrumb=PL&period=2006&javascript=true&navmapdisplayed=true& (accessed 13 July 2010).

Amin, A. 2002. Ethnicity and the multicultural city: Living with diversity. *Environment and Planning* 34: 959–980.

Babacan, A. and H. Babacan. 2007. Sustaining human security. *The International Journal of Environmental, Cultural, Economic and Social Sustainability* 3 (1): 115–122.

Babacan, A. and H. Babacan. 2006. Fear politics, new racism and the Cronulla riots. *Migration Action* 28 (1): 15–20.

Babacan, H. 2007. Education and social cohesion. In *Social cohesion in Australia*, eds J. Jupp and J. Nieuwenhuysen, 142–157. Melbourne: Cambridge University Press.

Babacan, H. and D. Hollinsworth. 2010. *Confronting racism in communities: Report*. Brisbane: Centre for Multicultural Pastoral Care.

Babacan, H., N. Gopalkrishnan and A. Babacan. 2009. *Situating racism: The local, national, and the global*. Cambridge: Cambridge Scholars Press.

Babacan, H. and N. Gopalkrishnan. 2008. Racism and asylum seeker policies. In *Asylum seekers: International perspectives on interdiction and deterrence*, eds L. Briskman and A. Babacan, 143–157. Cambridge: Cambridge Scholars Press.

Bloch, B. A. and T. Dreher. 2009. Resentment and reluctance: Working with everyday diversity and everyday racism in southern Sydney. *Journal of Intercultural Studies* 30 (2): 193–209.

Castles, S. and A. Davidson. 2000. *Citizenship and migration: Globalization and the politics of belonging*. Houndmills: Macmillan Press.

Cheongsam, P. H., R. Edwards, H. Goulbourne and J. Solomos. 2007. Immigration, social cohesion and social capital: A critical review. *Critical Social Policy* 27 (2): 24–49.

Clyne, M. 2005. The use of exclusionary language to manipulate opinion: John Howard, asylum seekers and the re-emergence of political incorrectness in Australia. *Journal of Language and Politics* 4 (2): 173–196.

Colenso, P. 2005. Education and social cohesion: Developing a framework for education sector reform in Sri Lanka. *Compare* 35 (4): 411–428.

Corlett, D. 2002. Asylum seekers and the new racism. *Dissent* 8: 46–47.

Council of Europe. 2001. *Diversity and cohesion: New challenges for the integration of immigrants and minorities*. Directorate of Social Affairs and Health, www.coe.int/t/dg3/migration/documentation/Series_Community_Relations/Diversity_Cohesion_en.pdf (accessed 2 May 2011).

Council of Europe. 1997. *In from the margins: A contribution to the debate on culture and development in Europe*. Strasbourg, www.coe.int/t/dg4/cultureheritage/culture/resources/Publications/InFromTheMargins_EN.pdf (accessed 1 May 2011).

Crawford, C. 2003. *Towards a common approach to thinking about and measuring social inclusion*. Paper presented at the Social Inclusion Research Conference, Ottowa. The Canadian Council on Social Development and Human Resources Development.

DIAC. 2011. *The people of Australia: Australia's Multicultural Policy*. Department of Immigration and Citizenship, www.immi.gov.au/living-in-australia/a-multicultural-australia/multicultural-policy/ (accessed 10 May 2011).

—. 2010. *Life in Australia*: *Australian values: Fact sheet no. 7*. Department of Immigration and Citizenship, www.immi.gov.au /media/fact-sheets/07values.htm (accessed 3 May 2011).

—. 2007. *Fact sheet: More than 60 years of post-war migration*. Department of Immigration and Citizenship, www.immi.gov.au/media/fact-sheets/04fifty.htm (accessed 3 April 2011).

Dunn, K., J. Forrest, I. Burnley and A. McDonald. 2004. Constructing racism in Australia. *Australian Journal of Social Issues* 39 (4): 409–430.

Durkheim, E. 1956. *Education and sociology,* trans. S. D. Fox. Glencoe, Ill: The Free Press.

Foucault, M. 1988. *Madness and civilization: A history of insanity in the age of reason*. New York: Vintage Books.

Forrest, R. and A. Kearns. 2001. Social cohesion, social capital and the neighbourhood. *Urban Studies* 38: 2125–43.

Fraser, C. and M. Islam. 2000. Social identification and political preferences for one nation: The role of symbolic racism. *Australian Journal of Psychology* 52 (3): 131–7.

Furedi, F. 2005. *Politics of fear: Beyond left and right*. London: Continuum International Publishing.

Giddens, A. and P. W. Sutton. 2010. *Sociology: Introductory readings*. Cambridge: Polity Press.

Gopalkrishnan, N. 2007. Neo-liberalism and infeartainment: What does a state do? In *Racisms in the new world order: Realities of cultures, colours and identity,* eds N. Gopalkrishnan and H. Babacan, 22–33. Cambridge: Cambridge Scholars Press.

Hage, G. 1998. *White nation: Fantasies of white supremacy in a multicultural society*. Sydney: Pluto Press.

Hall, S. 1997. Representation: Cultural representations and signifying practices. London: Sage Publications.
Hollinsworth, D. 2006. *Race and racism in Australia,* 3rd edn. Melbourne: Thomson and Social Science Press.
Hooghe, M. 2007. Social capital and diversity: Generalized trust, social cohesion and regimes of diversity. *Canadian Journal of Political Science* 40: 709–732.
HREOC. 2004. *Ismae-listen: National consultations on eliminating prejudice against Arab and Muslim Australians.* Sydney: Human Rights and Equal Opportunity Commission.
Jayasuriya, L. 2003. *Australian multiculturalism: Past, present and future.* Paper presented at ManagingDiversity Conference, 1–3 October 2003, Melbourne.
Jeannotte, S. 2000. *Social cohesion around the world: An international comparison of definitions and issues.* Department of Canadian Heritage, www.fas.umontreal/pol/cohesionsociale (accessed 28 May 2010).
Jenson, J. 2007. Identifying the links: Social cohesion and culture. *Canadian Journal of Communication* 27: 141–151.
Jupp, J., A. McRobbie and B. York. 1991. *Settlement needs of small, newly arrived ethnic groups.* Canberra: AGPS.
Kershan, A. J. 2005. The 1905 Aliens Act. *History Today* 55 (3): 13–19.
McPherson, M. 2010. "I integrate, therefore I am": Contesting the normalizing discourse of integrationism through conversations with refugee women. *Journal of Refugee Studies* 23 (4): 546–570.
Ouseley, H. 2004. Forget this phoney debate, it's time to confront racism. *The Guardian,* 10 April 2004, www.guardian.co.uk/politics/2004/apr/10/society.race (accessed 10 May 2011).
Pedersen, A., J. Beven, I. Walker and B. Griffiths. 2004. Attitudes towards indigenous Australians: The role of empathy and guilt. *Journal of Community and Applied Social Psychology* 14: 233–49.
Pickering, S. 2001. Common sense and original deviancy: News discourses and asylum seekers in Australia. *Journal of Refugee Studies* 14 (2): 167–185.
Poynting, S. and G. Noble. 2004. Living with racism: The experience and reporting by Arab and Muslim Australians of discrimination, abuse and violence since September 2001. Report to the Human Rights and Equal Opportunity Commission, 19 April 2004, www.hreoc.gov.au/racial_discrimination/isma/research/index.html (accessed 3 September 2010).

Robin, C. 2004. The politics and antipolitics of fear. *Raritan* (New Brunswick) 23 (4).

Simmel, G. 1950. *The sociology of George Simmel*. New York: Free Press.

Soroka, S. N., R. Johnston and K. Banting. 2007. Ties that bind? Social cohesion and diversity in Canada. In *Belonging? Diversity, recognition and shared citizenship in Canada*, eds K. Banting, T. J. Courchene and F. L. Seidle, 561–600. Montreal: IRPP.

Southphommasane, T. 2005. Grounding multicultural citizenship: From minority rights to civic pluralism. *Journal of Intercultural Studies* 26 (4): 401–416.

Vasta, E. 2007. *Accommodating diversity: Why current critiques of multiculturalism miss the point*. Working paper no. 53. Oxford: Centre on Migration, Policy and Society, University of Oxford.

Westwood, S. and A. Phizacklea. 2000. *Trans-nationalism and the politics of belonging*. London: Routledge.

Wise, A. 2006. Hope and belonging in a multicultural suburb. *Journal of Intercultural Studies* 26 (1–2): 171–86.

Zournazi, M. and G. Hage. 2002. On the side of life, joy and the capacity of being: A conversation with Ghassan Hage. In *Hope: New philosophies for change*, ed. M. Zournazi. London: Routledge.

CHAPTER EIGHT

COUNTERING TERRORISM THROUGH COMMUNITY ENGAGEMENT

HUSSEIN TAHIRI

Australia is increasingly becoming part of a globalised society, and as a country, it cannot afford not to become involved in this process, as it may not be able to prosper in isolation. Therefore, Australia needs to interact with the rest of the world and participate in international affairs. In fact, Australia has become one of the key players in economic and political international developments. What happens in other parts of the world can, and does, affect Australia directly.

Even if Australia opted not to actively participate in international affairs, the composition of its society would require it to do so. Australia is a multicultural society and people of many different ethnicities, nationalities and faiths have chosen to live here. As such, it does not have the option of isolation from the rest of the world; it is bound to be affected by events occurring in other parts of the world. Being a part of the global world brings with it opportunities and challenges. One of the challenges that Australia has faced is the threat of terrorism.[1]

Australia has not experienced the level of terrorist threats which are prevalent in many other countries. However, it does not mean that Australia is, or has been, immune from terrorism. In the 1970s and 1980s a number of groups such as Yugoslav separatists, Ananda Marga, Justice Commandos of the Armenian Genocide, Palestinian groups and anti-nuclear activists were involved in a number of terrorist incidents. From 1970 to 1985 there were 34 terrorism-related incidents in Australia (Hocking 1993: 202–204). The most serious incidents were the 1978 explosion in which a bomb was placed in a rubbish bin outside the Hilton

[1] I acknowledge that terrorism is not specific to any ethnic, national, religious or ideological group. However, in this paper terrorism refers to individuals or groups who exploit the religion of Islam to justify their acts of terrorism.

Hotel in Sydney and killed three people, and the assassination of the Turkish Consul-General in 1980 that led to the deaths of two people (Hocking 1993: 95, 203).

After several decades Australia is now facing a different kind of threat from terrorism. In the 1970s and 1980s its security was threatened by nationalist groups whose activities extended to Australia while their main focus remained in their original countries. In other words, Australia served as a venue for terrorists. However, for the new generation of terrorists, Australia is no more a venue but is the target. This threat is ideological and does not recognise any geographical border. The frontline could be anywhere in the world and the target could be any person, government security agency or official, or innocent population. As C. J. de Poot et al. stated, referring to "homegrown" terrorist threats to the Netherlands, their enemy could be anywhere in the world and they are willing to target Western interests anywhere without making much distinction between domestic and foreign targets (de Poot et al. 2011: 104).

As a result of this "unique" threat there have been a number of arrests in Australia in the last several years. In 2004, Jack Roche was found guilty of conspiring to blow up the Israeli embassy.[2] In 2006, Faheem Khalid Lodhi was sentenced to 20 years jail for undertaking preparations for a terrorist act.[3] In 2005 and 2006, Abdul Nacer Benbrika was arrested, along with 12 others in Victoria and nine in New South Wales, and charged with a range of terrorism-related offences. Seven of those arrested in Victoria were convicted in the Victorian Supreme Court for offences which included "being a member of a terrorist organisation", "directing a terrorist organisation" and "provide resources to a terrorist organisation" (Australasian Legal Information Institute 2011). Of those arrested in New South Wales, five were convicted on similar charges (Brown 2010).

In August 2009, five people in Melbourne were arrested (Operation Neath) and charged for allegedly "planning to carry out a suicide terrorist attack" on an Australian military base using "automatic weapons" in "a sustained attack on military personnel until they themselves were killed". In December 2010, a jury found three of them guilty of planning an attack on the Holsworthy Army Base in Sydney (Ross and Anderson 2010). Thus

---

[2] Jailed for nine years. R v Roche [2005] WASCA 4. Note that the conviction was under pre-2002 legislation (Crimes Act s.86, as at 2000) and not under terrorism legislation.

[3] Also found guilty on two other charges. Sentenced on 23/8/2006 to 20 years jail, with 15 year non-parole period. R v Lodhi [2006] NSWSC 691. Several related NSW Supreme Court cases 2005+ - see AustLII.

far, a total of 21 Australian citizens have been convicted of terrorism charges (Porter and Kebbell 2010: 1).

Of course, these people do not turn to violence overnight. They go through a process of radicalisation and extremism. The challenge is to understand this process so that effective intervention and prevention strategies can be identified. The threat of terrorism cannot be effectively prevented or minimised without addressing this complexity and tackling the causes and the process of radicalisation and extremism.

Research on terrorism to date indicates that there is no one specific factor or factors contributing to terrorism.[4] It is generally acknowledged that terrorism is multi-faceted and complex so a variety of strategies needs to be employed to reduce the threat. Unfortunately, as Noah Feldman put it, "the 'war on terror' approach focused on consolidating states' coercive power" (Feldman 2004: 12).

The traditional approach to terrorism has been "top down" through a paramilitary approach involving security agencies and intelligence personnel. This approach is vital but only as a secondary prevention, that is, to prevent those who have already decided to use terrorism as a means to achieve their aims. In such a situation, intelligence and security agencies might be the only means available to make sure the community is not harmed by terrorists.

However, in the current complex environment, it has become very difficult to prevent someone who is thinking of sacrificing himself/herself by committing acts of terror. Coercive powers might not be effective in such a situation. Indeed, the experience over the last nine years has proven that coercive methods have not been effective in suppressing terrorism. So, the root causes and processes of radicalisation and extremism which could lead to terrorism should be targeted. As John Horgan stated:

> If "understanding" terrorism is our objective, then we need to be clear on where terrorism comes from, how it emerges, develops and ends. To achieve this objective, and perhaps to then attempt to discover how such understanding might better inform policy, we must be open to accepting the realities of our own actions in attempting to suppress terrorism. (Horgan 2005: 166–167)

In order to prevent terrorism we must be able to understand what inspires it. We should be able to see things through terrorists' eyes and

---

[4] For an example, see de Poot, C. J., A. Sonnenschein, M. R. J. Soudijn, J .G. M. Bijen and M. W. Verkuylen. 2011. *Jihadi terrorism in the Netherlands: A description based on closed criminal investigations*, WODC, National Police Services. The Hague: Boom juridische uitgevers.

understand why and how they justify their cause – why their ideas are attractive to some of their fellow Muslims.[5] Only then will we be able to design strategies to counter them.

Some terrorist groups have been exploiting the religion of Islam as a justification for committing acts of terror. The case of Mohammed Taheri-Azar who was arrested and charged with intentionally hitting people with a car on the campus of the University of North Carolina at Chapel Hill, injuring nine people, is an example of how religion is used to justify terrorism. In his letter to the police, he wrote:

> I am a servant of Allah… [I] graduated in December 2005 with a bachelor's degree in psychology and philosophy with Allah's help. I do not wish to pursue my career as a student any further because I have no desire to amass the impermanent and temporary fame and material wealth this world has to offer. However I made the decision to continue my studies and to graduate from the University of North Carolina at Chapel Hill so that the world will know that Allah's servants are very intelligent.
>
> Due to the killing of believing men and women under the direction of the United States government, I have decided to take advantage of my presence on United States soil on Friday, March 3, 2006 to take the lives of as many Americans and American sympathizers as I can in order to punish the United States for their immoral actions around the world.
>
> In the Qur'an, Allah states that the believing men and women have permission to murder anyone responsible for the killing of other believing men and women. I know that the Qur'an is a legitimate and authoritative holy scripture since it is completely validated by modern science and also mathematically encoded with the number 19 beyond human ability. After extensive contemplation and reflection, I have made the decision to exercise the right of violent retaliation that Allah has given me to the fullest extent to which I am capable at present.
> (*Herald-Sun* [Durham, Chapel Hill, NC], 24 March 2006)

Are we equipped to deal with such cases and prevent others from falling into this trap of vengeance in the name of God?

It should be emphasised that religion in itself is not a problem. In fact, leaked MI5 research showed "a strong religious identity was an effective bulwark against terrorism" (Bartlett and Birdwell 2010: 9). However, there

[5] Again, I acknowledge that terrorism is not specific to any ethnic, national, religious or ideological group. However, in this paper terrorism refers to individuals or groups who exploit the religion of Islam to justify their acts of terrorism.

are a small number of people who use religion for their political purpose. Their numbers might currently be insignificant but the social consequences could be huge. Especially in a multicultural society such as Australia, it could have a significant impact on community cohesion and harmony.

Australia has generally enjoyed good community relations within and across its diverse communities. Nevertheless, one can never be sure that it will be immune from terrorist threats. There were reports that Iraqi veteran terrorists were being sent overseas to conduct terrorist activities. Maj. Gen. Achraf Rifi, general director of the Internal Security Forces in Lebanon, said, "If any country says it is safe from this [export of terrorists from Iraq], they are putting their heads in the sand" (Moss and Mekhennet 2007).

On 28 May 2007, *The New York Times* published an article which read:

> When Muhammad al-Darsi got out of prison in Libya last year after serving time for militant activities, he had one goal: killing Americans in Iraq… A recruiter he found on the Internet arranged to meet him on a bridge in Damascus, Syria. But when he got there, Mr. Darsi, 24, said the recruiter told him he was not needed in Iraq… He asked Mr. Darsi to join them and blow himself up in a crowd of tourists at Queen Alia Airport in Amman.
> (Moss and Mekhennet 2007)

Anecdotal evidence indicates that there are people in Australia who have expressed sympathies for overseas causes and radical ideas and they might entertain the idea of joining "jihad" overseas. In fact, there has been a claim that up to 40 Australians have joined the fighting in Somalia (Cilluffo et al. 2010: 7). If these people were told that they were not needed overseas and they were rather asked to carry out their "jihad" here in Australia, we would be facing a great danger. The case of Zazi, a legal resident of the United States, is a clear example of this. Zazi went to Afghanistan to join the Taliban where he was trained by al Qaeda and then sent back to the United States. After his arrest in September 2009, he admitted that he had planned to attack the New York subway system (Cilluffo et al. 2010: 4). In fact, a new al-Qaeda strategy is to ask its members and sympathisers in the West not to go to confrontational places any more and to carry out their "jihad" where they are (Inspire Magazine 5 2011).

Furthermore, as indicated earlier, there have been a number of terrorist-related cases in Australia and Australia is potentially exposed to the threat of terrorism from a few fronts. All evidence points to a non-coercive method as the key component of countering terrorism if we are to be strategic in our approach to preventing terrorism. A United Nations (UN) report states that many states have recognised that military and other repressive methods alone are not enough and in some cases are counter-productive for preventing terrorism. They are therefore increasing their attention to non-coercive approaches with the aim of preventing potential terrorists from resorting to violent in the first place (Counter Terrorism Implementation Task Force, UN).

Thus, mitigating the threat of terrorism necessitates a more proactive approach – an approach that will deal with the issue before it becomes a major problem. Such an approach requires engaging those who might pose a potential risk and also involving the community to help with the engagement of those people who might pose a risk. The community has a key role to play in long-term counter terrorism strategies (Briggs 2010: 972, 981). As Wong Kan Seng (2009: 18) stated, terrorism is ultimately defeated by the people not by governments.

Community Engagement

In discussing how to counter terrorism through community engagement, it is imperative to understand what we mean by community, what is community engagement and why we need to engage the community.

"Community" is a very broad term used to define groups of people, who can be stakeholders, interest groups, citizens groups etc. A community may be a geographic one, a community of shared interest, or a community of affiliation or identity (Bartkowiak-Theron and Corbo Crehan 2010: 9–11). While community can be defined from the local to the global, for our purposes here community is defined as a geographic community in Australia. This definition includes all the individuals and groups in a particular area, regardless of how they may or may not identify with others in the community or with the community as a whole. It is within this broad definition of community that we need to navigate our community engagement process.

The International Association for Public Participation (IAP2) defines "community engagement" as: "any process that involves the community in problem-solving or decision-making and uses community input to make better decisions" (Twyford et al. 2006: 19).

Community engagement thus means involving the community in decision making, information sharing and problem-solving by using their input to make more informed decisions. This includes decisions that directly impact upon living, working, playing, studying, using services and doing business. Engaging with the community is more than just consulting; it includes collaboration and empowerment (City of Charles Sturt, Adelaide).

Different levels of community engagement can be used to suit the particular project and community needs. Community engagement can be employed to:

- Inform the community about a certain issues
- Consult the community to inform the development of policies, listen to and acknowledge their concerns and provide feedback on how community engagement/public feedback influenced the decision
- Involve the community to make sure that their aspirations are directly reflected in planning and policies and ensure that their issues and concerns are understood and considered when developing policies
- Collaborate with the community through the development of partnerships to formulate options and provide recommendations by incorporating their advice and recommendations to the maximum extent possible
- Empower the community through building their capacity and implementing their decisions

(Department of Sustainability and Environment 2005: 10)

Community engagement is a two-way process that requires both government and the community to take action following engagement where that action is appropriate in light of all the circumstances and information available. Therefore, community engagement is not just casual interaction with individuals or a group within a community. It is also not just a conversation or listening to the community. It is interaction with a clear, shared purpose that requires each of us to bring our holistic selves to the conversation, allows us to be honoured for our knowledge and contribution, and enables us to walk away with a clear understanding of the "what" and "why" of engagement. In this sense, engagement has an implicit message of connection, joint creation and mutual responsibility (Twyford et al. 2006: 19).

Why Do We Need to Engage the Community?

Community engagement has formed the core business of many non-government organisations such as aid agencies for decades. However, community engagement as a core business strategy is a new phenomenon for governments. In democratic societies there is an increasing expectation by the community for governments to be responsible, transparent, accountable and effective. In response to this expectation, governments are increasingly adopting community engagement as a tool to involve the community in decision making.

Community engagement delivers tangible benefits to the government and the community by allowing governments to make effective decisions based on the expertise and knowledge within a community for identifying local and emerging issues and developing more responsive services. Community involvement in informing policies and projects gives more legitimacy to government decision-making processes, minimises misinformation, reduces risk and helps to build community trust in the government.

Furthermore, community engagement as a key element of community policing provides a tool to encourage and develop trust and relationships between the police and the community. Strengthening community relationships is critical in providing police with information to pursue offenders and prevent crimes (Putt 2010: 28).

In addition, there is an overwhelming body of research showing that community engagement is the most effective way to reduce general crime. Research indicates that:

- Effective police operations are dependent upon public support in terms of the provision of essential intelligence to the police and for respecting law and order in general.
- Positive community perceptions of police legitimacy have been linked to low levels of crime.
- Traditional methods of addressing crime concerns such as increasing police numbers were found to be unsuccessful at effecting long-term crime reduction.
- Initiatives created to encourage the development and maintenance of police-community partnerships make police practice more responsive and relevant to community problems and needs.

(Segrave and Ratcliffe 2004: 2)

A report on a review of crimes and communities describes the public as a very important weapon in dealing with crime. It states, "If people always reported what they know to the police, the local criminals could not continue to operate" (Casey 2008).

Also, research on terrorism increasingly highlights community engagement as the best way to prevent extremism and combat terrorism. A number of research projects support the notion of community engagement in countering terrorism[6] but this should be done in a way that does not

---

[6] Pickering, Sharon et al. 2007. *Counter terrorism policing and culturally diverse communities*, Final report;

create division and tension within the community. While many governments might speak of community involvement to provide intelligence, this should not be the primary purpose of engagement. Community engagement should aim at building trust, rather than be based solely on gathering intelligence (Pickering et al. 2007: 24).

Countering Terrorism through Community Engagement

It is often thought that radicals and extremists are isolated from the rest of the community and there is not much that community engagement can achieve in this area. This might be the case at advanced stages of radicalisation and extremism but most radicals and extremists are still part of the community and they have interaction with some sections of the community at pre-radicalisation or its early stages. Loiuse E. Porter and Mark R. Kebbell (2010: 15) state that the majority of 21 convicted terrorist in Australia were married, many had children and most had some form of employment. They had some sort of attachment to society. Isolation increased when radicalisation progressed and intensified. Thus, community engagement can play a vital role at least in pre-radicalisation or early stages of radicalisation.

Community engagement should focus on addressing social factors leading to alienation and marginalisation, particularly of young people. Research from Western Europe, the Middle East and South Asia all suggests that even if increased feelings of marginalisation from mainstream society are inadvertent, the policies that add to these feelings will not only fail to generate any tangible increase in security from terrorist violence, but they might even exacerbate the risk that such policies are designed to reduce.[7] Involvement in terrorist behaviour is, as

---

BIRR Initiative. 2010. *The way forward: An Islamic mentoring guide to building and resisting radicalisation*, 30 May 2010;

Pratchett, Lawrence, Leila Thorp, Melvin Wingfield and Vivian Lowndes. 2010. *Preventing support for violent extremism through community interventions: A review of the evidence,* Final report, March 2010. De Montfort University.

[7] For example, see Pickering, S. 2002. *Women, policing and resistance in Northern Ireland*. Belfast: Beyond the Pale Publications;

Taylor, M. and E. Quayle. 1994. *Terrorist lives*. London: Brassey's;

Wright, S. 1981. A multivariate time series analysis of the Northern Ireland conflict 1969–76. In *Behavioural and quantative perspectives on terrorism*, eds S. Wright, Y. Alexander and J. Gleason, 283–328. New York: Pergamon;

Kellen, K. 1990. Ideology and rebellion: Terrorism in West Germany. In *Origins of terrorism: Psychologies, ideologies, theologies, states of mind*, ed. W. Reich. New York: Cambridge University Press;

noted by the psychologist John Horgan, an incremental process that reflects "a slow, but real, marginalization away from conventional society … a sense of increasing disillusionment with alternative avenues [to violence] developing in conjunction with an increasing involvement in activities that culminate in having eventually become a terrorist" (Horgan 2005: 95).

Community engagement should also address the social disadvantages which make individuals and groups vulnerable to terrorist recruitment. Speckhard (2007) claims, "Unemployment, discrimination, no sense of belonging or positive identification with the society they live in make them [young people] vulnerable to alternative identities that terrorist organisations promote". She elaborates:

> We unwittingly create circumstances that greatly expand the pool of potential recruits when we fail to address the societal factors leading to individual vulnerability and societal support that make these groups impossible to extinguish, and in fact seems to make them replenish themselves faster than we can stop them. (Speckhard 2007)

John Taylor (2010), referring to the terrorist incident in Mumbai, India, on 26 November 2008, states:

> At least one of the terrorists, once caught, claimed that he had been sold by his father to Lashkar-i-Taiba recruiters for a bounty. He was then told that by following the leader's directions, completing training, and then executing their attack in India, that his family would receive benefit. The terrorists had little education and little experience in the modern world.

While lack of education and other disadvantages might put a person in a vulnerable position to be recruited by terrorist groups, not all terrorists have a disadvantaged background, as is generally thought.

There have been terrorists who were well educated, came from relatively well-off families and were considered well integrated. Peter Bergen and Bruce Hoffman state that evidence shows that many terrorists are well educated and have come from well-off families. Poverty, illiteracy

---

Branche, Raphaëlle. 2001. *La Torture et l'armée pendant la Guerre d'Algérie*. Series: La suite des temps. Paris: Gallimard;
Kaarthikeyan, Shri D. R. 2005. Root causes of terrorism? A case study of the Tamil insurgency and the LTTE. In *Root causes of terrorism: Myths, reality and ways forward*, ed. T. Bjørgo, 131–140. London: Routledge;
Wright-Neville, D. 2004. Australia's counter-terrorism laws and the assault on politics. In *Human rights 2003: The year in review*, ed. T. Davis. Clayton: Monash University.

and unemployment are not their motivation for resorting to terrorism. In fact, the modern method of terrorism requires them to be technologically savvy and have a good grasp of the world and the society they live in so that they can move around without attracting attention (Bergen and Hoffman 2010: 15–16). Therefore, it should not be assumed that poverty, marginalisation and alienation are the sole contributing factors for individuals becoming vulnerable to terrorism recruitment. Other factors such as ideology can play a pivotal role. So, addressing societal factors in our community engagement might not be sufficient. We should also challenge terrorists at the ideological level.

Governments, through their community engagement programs, should make it more difficult for terrorist groups to appeal to potential recruits on ideological grounds. This could be very effective in preventing extremism and radicalisation leading to terrorism. Al-Qaeda tends to exploit this ideological approach well. In many of its publications and media releases it wages an ideological battle against the West and its other enemies to justify its physical violence. For instance, a video released in September 2008 titled "The World is the Word of Swords" was supposed to give the details of preparations for the attack on the Danish Embassy in Islamabad, Pakistan. Instead, Abu Yahya al-Libi, one of al-Qaeda's leading religious authorities, dedicated the bulk of the 64-minute video to ideological war against al-Qaeda's enemies, explaining how Islam has been undermined by these enemies (Burton and Stewart 2008). In fact, propaganda to disseminate al-Qaeda's ideology is crucial to the terrorist organisation. It is claimed that al-Qaeda wages 90% of its battle in the media (Bergen and Hoffman 2010: 20), most of which is ideological battle with the West. Above all, it is this ideological appeal that provides al-Qaeda with recruits.

Evidence shows that terrorist groups use narratives supported by selected evidence from religious text to try to convince people to accept their cause and be recruited (de Poot et al. 2011: 49–53). Of the 21 people convicted of terrorism in Australia, 15 openly stated that their religion supported "jihad" and violence against those who did not share the same religious views (Porter and Kebbell 2010: 11). Thus, countering ideological support for terrorism should be a key strategy in responding to the current wave of terrorism and steps should be taken to produce an ideological counter strategy (Ali 2008: 127).

A key element of community engagement should be to present counter narratives. The Building Identity and Resisting Radicalisation Initiative (BIRR) recommends that the extremists and their propaganda should be challenged with counter-ideological narratives (BIRR Initiative 2010; 14). Professor Lawrence Pratchett and his colleagues list community engagement programs that challenge terrorists' ideology among the most successful interventions to prevent support for violent extremism in the name of religion (Pratchett et al. 2010: 8).

Of course, governments are not in a position to do this task on their own. A UN report states that states alone do not have resources to counter radicalisation and violent extremism. Civil societies and local communities have a range of tools and resources which are not available to governments and they might have access to sections of the community that the governments do not have. They can help with countering extremist ideologies and promoting peaceful dialogue. In addition, they can recognise early radicalisation trends in the community. The state, therefore, needs to enter into partnership with civil societies and local communities. Working with such organisations enhances trust and transparency and strengthens social cohesion (Counter Terrorism Implementation Task Force, UN).

The Australian Government has recognised this issue and expects the community to play a role in this matter. An Australian Government representative at a conference in 2007 stated that while government has a role, it is ultimately the friends and families of those who are at risk of radicalisation who are in a better position to identify and prevent the process of radicalisation (Porter and Kebbell 2010: 18).

However, it might be problematic to place responsibility with Muslim communities to combat radicalisation and extremism as this might create an assumption that Muslim communities themselves are the locus of terrorism (Spalek and Imtoual 2007: 194). Anecdotal evidence indicates that many people in Muslim communities do not think that it is their job to get involved in counter-terrorism initiatives as, like any other citizens, they are busy with their life and have nothing to do with terrorism. It is obvious that the overwhelming majority of Muslims has nothing to do with the acts of a tiny minority within their midst who misinterpret and misuse their religion to justify violence, and they should not be blamed for the acts of the very few. Placing responsibility with the Muslim communities does not and should not mean that they are blamed for acts of violence committed by some rogue elements within their communities; it simply means that when it comes to religious and counter-ideological narratives, it would not be appropriate for the government to intervene in Muslims' internal religious affairs and tell the Muslims what is right or wrong. Furthermore, governments have no legitimacy and authority in this area, nor should they get involved in theological debates.

Muslim communities are in a better position to do this and they should have a key role to challenge terrorists and their ideology, with government playing a supporting role. As Jamie Bartlett and Jonathan Birdwell (2010:

30) outlined, "The Government's role must shift from that of a policy provider, to an enabler and facilitator that helps to build capacity and then steps back".

Muslims would gain significantly from challenging terrorists at the ideological level. Firstly, terrorists misuse the religion of Islam for their own political purpose and in the process link the religion of Islam with violence. Secondly, after each terrorist act, Muslims experience discrimination and abuse from certain sections of the community. Thirdly, Muslims, like any other members of the community, are the target of the terrorist violence. So, Muslims would benefit greatly by countering extremism and radicalisation leading to violence and they could play a pivotal role in combating those who misuse and abuse their religion.

Of course, community engagement is not a one-way street. Engaging Australian multicultural communities would not be enough to achieve a cohesive society. The mainstream Anglo-Australian community needs to be part of this engagement. A lot of work still needs to be done on this front. A study published in 2008 by the University of Western Sydney indicated that racism remained high in Australia. Four out of ten Australians believed that some ethnic groups did not belong in Australia and one in ten had overtly racist views (*Herald Sun* 14 October 2008). A decade-long national study published in February 2011 found that 48.6% of Australians expressed anti-Muslim sentiments (ABC, 23 February 2011). In the context of community harmony and cohesion, this is a serious concern. These negative views could be perceived by some sections of the community as that they are not wanted in Australia and this could well feed into terrorist narratives.

Therefore, a comprehensive community engagement strategy across all sectors of the community to promote community collaboration at various levels should be adopted. Such a strategy could play a key role in preventing radicalisation and extremism leading to terrorism.

Conclusion

The above discussion indicates that terrorism is a complex issue and needs a multitude of approaches. There is no denying that a coercive approach has to be taken at appropriate times when there is threat to the community. Nevertheless, as the International Crisis Group stated:

> The government needs to recognise that laws are not a panacea. This is not a problem that can be fixed by a new intelligence law or a strengthened anti-terrorism law. The effort has to start in communities, by reducing the receptivity to extremist messages, finding alternative activities and role

> models for young men in their twenties in certain targeted areas, and showing that other approaches produce concrete benefits.
> (International Crisis Group 201: 22)

There is general consensus that community engagement is the most effective approach in preventing terrorism, especially for long-term and durable solutions. Rachel Briggs (2010) states, "community engagement is central to an effective response to international terrorism and has earned its place in counter terrorism strategies for the foreseeable future". Community engagement in countering terrorism has become so important that Detective Superintendent John Prunty, who had extensive involvement in the UK's terrorism cases including the 7/7 bombings, said at a Senior Managers CT Forum on 4 July 2007, "If I had three million pounds I would spend two and half million in community engagement".

During the last several years there has been an increasing focus on community engagement, both generic and targeted, to reduce the threat of terrorism. The Australian Government has taken measures at various levels to prevent terrorism. However, until very recently the focus was mainly on secondary prevention (intelligence), preparedness and response. There was less focus on primary prevention – that is, to prevent the process of radicalisation and extremism happening in the first place. Australian governments, particularly the Victorian Government and Victoria Police, realising this fact, have changed their focus to primary prevention through community engagement.

In Australia, significant resources are being allocated to generic community engagement strategies to promote community harmony and cohesion in order to create a community resistant to terrorism. But are critics such as Jamie Bartlett and Jonathan Birdwell correct when they claim, "it is widely believed that Prevent [UK] has alienated Muslim communities, increased intercommunity tensions, and threatens to undo a number of good initiatives that contribute to community cohesion because of the link to counter terrorism" (Bartlett and Birdwell 2010: 10)? If this is the case, is Australia investing so much in an area that may be counter-productive? There is a need for further study in this area to see if such a claim can be substantiated.

Alternatively, should Australia adopt a targeted community engagement approach which focuses on vulnerable members of the community who are considered extremists or exposed to extremist ideas? If it does, how should it engage these individuals and groups and how should it be done so as not to have a negative impact on community relations? This area too needs further research.

To conclude, community engagement, although very important, should not be considered as the panacea for preventing or reducing the threat of terrorism. A holistic approach to the issue also requires a measured terrorism-related language, vigilant security forces, and counter terrorism policies and legislation proportional to the level of threat and not perceived as targeting any particular community. A balanced approach between various counter-terrorism initiatives should increase the potential for a meaningful engagement and effective outcomes.

References

ABC. 2011. *Nearly half of Australians are anti-Muslim: Study*, 23 February 2001, www.abc.net.au/news/stories/2011/02/23/3146427.htm (accessed 9 March 2011).

Ali, U. M. 2008. *Countering extremist ideologies in winning hearts and minds, embracing peace*. Singapore: Religious Rehabilitation Group.

Australasian Legal Information Institute. 2011. *R v Benbrika & Ors (2009) in the Supreme Court*, www.austlii.edu.au/au/cases/vic/VICSC/2009/21.html (accessed 22 May 2011).

Bartkowiak-Theron, I. and A. Corbo Crehan. 2010. The changing nature of communities: Implications for police and community policing. In *Community policing in Australia*, ed. A. J. Putt, 33–43. AIC Reports, Research and Public Policy Series 111.

Bartlett, J. and J. Birdwell. 2010. *From suspects to citizens: Preventing violent extremism in a big society*, www.demos.co.uk/files/From_Suspects_to_Citizens_web.pdf? 1279732377 (accessed 11 October 2010).

Bergen, P. and B. Hoffman. 2010. *Assessing the terrorist threat: A report of the Bipartisan Policy Center's National Security Preparedness Group*, 10 September 2010.

BIRR Initiative. 2010. *The way forward: An Islamic mentoring guide to building and resisting radicalisation*, 30 May 2010.

Briggs, R. 2010. Community engagement for counter terrorism: Lessons from the United Kingdom. *International Affairs* 86 (4): 971–981.

Brown, M. 2010. Five Sydney terrorists jailed. *The Age*, 15 February 2010, www.theage.com.au/national/five-sydney-terrorists-jailed-20100215-o1fo.html (accessed 22 May 2011).

Burton, F. and S. Stewart. 2008. *Al Qaeda and the tale of two battlespaces*, 1 October 2008. Stratfor.

Casey, L. 2008. *Engaging communities in fighting crime*,

www.cabinetoffice.gov.uk/media/cabinetoffice/corp/assets/publications/crime/cc_full_report.pdf (accessed 26 November 2010).

Cilluffo, F. J, J. B. Cozzens and M. Ranstorp. 2010. *Foreign fighters: Trends, trajectories and conflict zones*. Homeland Security Policy Institute, George Washington University.

City of Charles Sturt (Adelaide). 2011. *Community engagement model*, www.charlessturt.sa.gov.au/Portals/0/Community%20Engagement%20Model.pdf (accessed 3 June 2011).

Counter Terrorism Implementation Task Force, UN. 2011. *First report of the Working Group on Radicalisation and Extremism that Lead to Terrorism: Inventory of state programmes*, www.un.org/terrorism/pdfs/radicalization.pdf (accessed 27 May 2011).

Department of Sustainability and Environment. 2005. *Effective engagement: Building relationships with community and other stakeholders*: *Book 1, an instruction to engagement*. Melbourne: DSE.

De Poot, C. J., A.Sonnenschein, M. R. J. Soudijn, J. G .M Bijen and M. W. Verkuylen. 2011. *Jihadi terrorism in the Netherlands: A description based on closed criminal investigations*. WODC, National Police Services. The Hague: Boom juridische uitgevers.

Herald Sun. 2008. *Study unearths Australian racist views*, 14 October 2008, www.news.com.au/heraldsun/story/0,21985,24416160–662,00.html, (accessed 3 June 2011).

Herald-Sun (Durham, Chapel Hill, NC). 2006. *Mohammed Taheri-Azar's letter to police*, 24 March 2006, www.investigativeproject.org/documents/case_docs/248.pdf (accessed 1 June 2011).

Hocking, J. 1993. *Beyond terrorism: The development of the Australian security state*. St Leonards, NSW: Allen and Unwin.

Horgan, J. 2005. *The psychology of terrorism*. London: Routledge.

Inspire Magazine (al-Qaeda in Arabian Peninsula publication). 2011. *Inspire* 5: 1431.

International Crisis Group. 2011. *Indonesian Jihadism: Small groups, big plans*. Asia Report no. 204, 19 April 2011.

Kan Seng, W. 2009. The role of community and faith leaders. In *Countering radicalism: The next generation and challenges ahead,* ed. A. H. Bin Kader. Singapore: Taman Baccan.

Moss, M. and S. Mekhennet. 2007. Militants widen reach as terror seeps out of Iraq. *The New York Times*, 28 May 2007, www.nytimes.com/2007/05/28/world/middleeast/28exodus.html (accessed2 June 2011).

Noah Feldman, N. 2004. *What we owe Iraq: War and the ethic of nation building*. New Jersey: Princeton University Press.

Pickering, S., D. Wright-Neville, J. McCulloch and P. Lentini. 2007. *Counter terrorism policing and culturally diverse communities*. Canberra: Australian Institute of Criminology.

Porter, L. E. and M. R. Kebbell. 2010. *Radicalisation in Australia: Examining Australia's convicted terrorists' psychiatry, psychology and law*. Brisbane: Griffith University.

Pratchett, L., L. Thorp, M. Wingfield and V. Lowndes. 2010. *Preventing support for violent extremism through community interventions: A review of the evidence*. Leicester: De Montfort University.

Putt J., ed. 2010. *Community policing in Australia*. Australian Institute of Criminology (AIC) Reports, Research and Public Policy Series 111. Canberra: AIC.

Ross, N. and P. Anderson. 2010. Three Melbourne men guilty of planning terror attack on NSW army base. *Herald Sun*, 23 December 2010, www.heraldsun.com.au/news/victoria/three-melbourne-men-guilty-of-planning-terror-attack-on-nsw-army-base/story-e6frf7kx–1225975357525 (accessed 22 May 2011).

Segrave, M. and J. Ratcliffe. 2008. *Community policing: A descriptive overview*. Australian Institute of Criminology www.aic.gov.au/publications/other/2004-03-policing.pdf (accessed 24 March 2008).

Spalek, B. and A. Imtoual. 2007. Muslim communities and counter-terror responses: "Hard" approaches to community engagement in the UK and Australia. *Journal of Muslim Minority Affairs* 27 (2).

Speckhard, A. 2007. De-legitimizing terrorism: Creative engagement and understanding of the psycho-social processes involved in ideological support for terrorism. *Connections* winter 2007, http://theclaw.typepad.com/speckhard_vault/files/De-legitimizing_Terrorism.pdf (accessed 3 June 2011).

Taylor, J. 2010. *Lessons learned: Mumbai terror attack: Analyzing one attack in order to disrupt the next*, 18 August 2010, www.homeland1.com/homeland-security-columnists/john-taylor/articles/867818-lessons-learned-mumbai-terror-attack/ (accessed 19 September 2010).

Twyford, V., S. Waters, M. Hardy and J. Dengate. 2006. *Beyond public meetings: Connecting community engagement with decision-making*. Sydney: Vivien Twyford Communication Pty Limited.

CHAPTER NINE

SEARCHING FOR ALTERNATIVE SOLUTIONS

HUSSEIN TAHIRI AND ALPERHAN BABACAN

Immediately after the terrorist attack on the United States on 11 September 2001, there were speculations that the world would never be the same again. One wondered – surely there had been many other incidents that had been equally or much more tragic with many more casualties but that had not had a great impact on the world! Not long after, it became apparent that the world was actually going to change. It was true that other incidents had been equally or more tragic but they had occurred in countries that did not have the resources or power to effect changes around the world. In the case of September 11, the very authority, integrity, sovereignty and pride of the world's sole superpower was challenged, not by a state actor but by, until then, an insignificant terrorist group.

September 11 and subsequent developments in global terrorism have had a profound impact on the world in many ways. Soon after September 11, George W. Bush announced the "war on terror" which opened a broad front against an enemy that was not easy to identify and that could not be confined to a specific geographical location, and so the war-front became worldwide. The broad concept of the "war on terror" paved the way for attacks on Afghanistan and Iraq which further fuelled terrorism rage and provided terrorist groups with a strong rationale for recruiting and justifying their acts of terror. The concept of the "war on terror" also opened a broad social, political and cultural paradigm which led to changes in international and domestic laws, affected the liberty and freedom of citizens and undermined community harmony and cohesion.

The terrorist attacks of 11 September 2001 led to the emergence of new international laws and regulations to combat terrorism. In the absence of international laws to deal with individuals who were non-state actors, out of sympathy for the attack on the United States and under pressure from the US administration, Resolution 1373 was passed by the United

Nation's Security Council on 28 September 2001. The Resolution unequivocally condemned the terrorist attacks on the United States and expressed a determination to prevent all such acts. The Resolution further called on states to work together urgently to prevent and suppress terrorism.

This international obligation created by Resolution 1373, in conjunction with Bush's open call to the international community that "you are either with us or with the terrorists", and the development of an emergency mentality and sense of insecurity among the general population led to the development of some extraordinary policies and legislation in many countries, especially in the West.

The foregoing chapters of this book lead us to two broad conclusions regarding the impact of the "war on terror" in Australia.

Firstly, Australia as a willing participant of the "war on terror" participated in military actions and also introduced a raft of policies and legislation. The terrorist attacks in Bali in 2002, subsequent bombings of Australian targets in Indonesia and the London bombings of 2005 resulted in the introduction of further counter-terrorism policies and legislation which created new criminal offences and expanded the power of ASIO, the Australian Federal Police and local police, giving them extensive investigative, detention and questioning powers (Bronnitt and Stellios 2006). This prompted accusations that the Government's response was made in haste with no proper consideration or parliamentary input (Carne 2008). Civil libertarians and other human rights groups have pointed out that the Australian Government was overreacting and exaggerating the threat of terrorism by introducing legislative measures without any objective and actuarial measures of the risk of terrorism posed to Australia and how the legislation would prevent such risk. They pointed out that the rules and regulations which were preventative in nature departed fundamentally from the traditional criminal law and argued that in a democratic society limiting civil liberties could not be justified without a precise measurement of the actual threat.

Secondly, the Australian approach to counter terrorism linked the "war on terror" to the debates on immigration, refugees, asylum seekers and the Muslim community. As the debate on border security became more politicised, some sections of the media and the community came to link border security with immigration, refugees, asylum seekers and also to terrorism, creating an impression in the mainstream community that some migrant groups, Muslims and refugees were a potential threat to Australia's security (Hugo 2002: 39). Such discourses enabled the Australian Government to pursue a hard-line approach to the issue of asylum seekers as well as to the war on terror and to imply that social cohesion in Australia was under threat as some of the ethnic and religious minorities, especially those from Muslim backgrounds, were not willing or able to assimilate or integrate into Australian society.

In the debates on immigration, refugees and asylum seekers, Muslims were particularly singled out as having different values which were not compatible with mainstream Australian values. To add to this perception was the fact that in the post-2000 period, a majority of terrorist acts had been conducted by a tiny minority who claimed to be engaging in terrorism in the name of Islam. The language used to describe these people, particularly by the media and some government officials, resulted in the linking of Muslims with terrorism in the public domain (Pollak 2006).

A consequence of these public discourses for many Australian people who had limited interaction with Muslims or did not have much information about Islam was that Muslims and terrorism became synonymous and Muslims were therefore considered a security risk to Australia. Those members of the mainstream community were alarmed by the possibility that Muslims living among them could pose a security risk. The negative image of Muslims and Islam which had been created led to discrimination against Muslims which further contributed to their isolation and marginalisation. Many Muslims became disenchanted with their host society and began to question their sense of identity as Australians and Australian citizens. While some sections of the mainstream community considered Muslims as security risks and aggressors, the Muslims considered themselves as the victims of the identification of Islam with terrorism. There developed a mutual feeling of distrust which led to social tensions. The Cronulla riots in New South Wales is an example of the chronic tension within the community in Sydney to which the "war on terror" contributed its share.

Such developments cannot help social cohesion. Terrorist groups skilfully exploit such tensions and try to convince Muslims, particularly young people, that the West is waging war on Islam and Muslims, and this seems to be reinforced by the attitudes towards Muslims and their treatment in the West. Discrimination, isolation and marginalisation have led to an identity crisis for some Muslim youths. Terrorist groups and their propaganda have been able to use this tension within the community to radicalise and recruit some elements within the community to plan and carry out terrorist attacks within Australia. This has led to the phenomenon of "homegrown" terrorism, which has further worsened the relationship between Muslim communities and the mainstream Australian community.

This in turn has created alarm that if appropriate strategies are not developed, the situation could deteriorate.

Many Western countries have realised that tensions within and across the community can potentially lead to further radicalisation of some elements within the community. It has become evident that after ten years of using coercive power, the West has not been able to eradicate terrorism. In fact, a coercive, law-and-order and top-down approach to resolving this issue has led to a cycle of violence and mistrust. Therefore, a search for alternative approaches has begun throughout the world.

Australia like many other Western countries has begun to shift its focus from a coercive approach to tackling terrorism to a community engagement approach so as to prevent the process of radicalisation and extremism happening in the first place. The idea of a community engagement approach to terrorism is not new; it was adopted in Northern Ireland. Immediately after 9/11, that kind of approach was deemed ineffective for dealing with the new international threat (Briggs 2010: 971). However, after a decade of employing a coercive approach, the West has come to the realisation that the root causes of radicalisation and extremism leading to terrorism need to be addressed and comprehensive strategies need to be developed to reduce the threat.

The tackling of terrorism requires a holistic approach. A number of steps need to be taken to defuse tension and promote community harmony and cohesion. Firstly, Australian counter-terrorism policies and legislation need to be evaluated to assess their effectiveness in preventing terrorism, and all undue restrictions and limitations on civil liberties and process protections need to be removed. Policy and legislation should be proportional to the degree of the threat and grounded in a human-rights framework.

A comprehensive consultation is required with the community at all levels and with all other stakeholders. Consultation needs to be done in a depoliticised and objective manner. The mainstream community also needs to engage with Muslims and avoid behaviour that could be considered discriminatory. It would not be enough to expect Muslims to consider themselves part of Australian society. They also need to be accepted as such. Governments need to play an active and positive role in this regard.

The Muslim community has a significant role to play in this process. There are some elements, though very few, within the Muslim community who exploit the religion of Islam to justify their political objectives (de Poot et al. 2001: 49–53). They use Islamic religious text to justify their acts. Muslims need to stand up against those elements and condemn their violence in the strongest possible voice and refute their legitimacy by presenting counter narratives. This should not be done because Muslims are suspects and to be blamed for the acts of those few but because the destructive consequences of those who commit terrorism in the name of Islam do more to damage Muslims than anyone else.

Australia as a multicultural and diverse society can only prosper when its various subsections live together in harmony. Global terrorism has had a significant impact on this harmony, creating an environment where some sections of the community regard each other with suspicion and distrust. Fortunately, the Australian Government is beginning to change its counter-terrorism focus from a paramilitary approach to that of community engagement. This approach is believed to be effective if an effort is made to establish a true partnership between various sections of the community for working towards the security and wellbeing of all community members: an inclusive approach in which all subsets of the community feel they have a role in maintaining community harmony and cohesion.

References

Briggs, R. 2010. Community engagement for counter terrorism: Lessons from the United Kingdom. *International Affairs* 86 (4): 971–981.

Bronnitt, S. and J. Stellios. 2006. Sedition, security and human rights: Unbalanced law reform in the war on terror. *Melbourne University Law Review* 29: 923–960.

Carne, G. 2008. Hasten slowly: Urgency, discretion and review: A counter-terrorism legislative agenda and legacy. *Deakin Law Review* 13 (2): 49–99.

De Poot, C. J., A. Sonnenschein, M. R. J. Soudijn, J. G. M. Bijen and M. W. Verkuylen. 2011. *Jihadi terrorism in the Netherlands: A description based on closed criminal investigations*. WODC, National Police Services. The Hague: Boom juridische uitgevers.

Hugo, G. 2002. Australian immigration policy: The significance of the events of 11th September. *International Migration Review* 36 (1).

UN Security Council Resolution 1373. 2001, http://unispal.un.org/UNISPAL.NSF/0/392A001F254B4B9085256B4B00708233 (accessed 7 June 2011).

Pollak, R. 2006. The rumble down under. *The Nation* January 9/16, www.thenation.com/article/rumble-down-under (accessed 8 June 2011).

EDITORS AND CONTRIBUTORS

Editors

Dr Alperhan Babacan
Dr Babacan is the Program Director for the Juris Doctor Program at RMIT University. Dr Babacan holds degrees in Law and Political Science and a PhD from RMIT University. Dr Babacan has worked as a lawyer, a researcher and an academic. Dr Babacan's research mainly revolves around human rights law. He has published in national and international journals and has written several books on human rights.

Dr Hussein Tahiri
Dr Tahiri completed his PhD in political science at the University of Melbourne in 2001. He has worked as a lecturer in Middle Eastern politics. He is a commentator on Middle Eastern affairs and has widely published in the Australian and international media. Dr Tahiri is currently an Adjunct Research Associate at the School of Political and Social Inquiry at Monash University.

Contributors

Professor Hurriyet Babacan
Professor Babacan is the Director of the Cairns Institute at James Cook University. She has led numerous national and international research and development projects. She has recently been a member of two Council of Europe and OECD working parties. Professor Babacan has published nationally and internationally on the issues of health, welfare, multiculturalism, immigration, identity, social policy, gender, racism, settlement and community development.

Dr Robin Cameron
Dr Cameron is a Research Fellow in Human Security at the Global Cities Institute. He has previously held positions as a lecturer in Criminology at the University of Melbourne and in International Relations at Deakin University and holds a PhD in International Relations from the Australian National University. Dr Cameron is working on a book that examines the

role of foreign policy and national discourses in shaping domestic order and social control.

Dr Donald Feaver

Dr Feaver is an Associate Professor at the Graduate School of Business and Law, RMIT University. In addition to teaching international public and private law subjects, his research interests include the fast-evolving multilateral regulatory system. Dr Feaver has published numerous articles in leading international journals relating to the design and operation of international regulatory arrangements such as the World Trade Organization's anti-competition agreements and the UN's climate change regime. His interest in the international regulation of counter-terrorism activity is centred around how it can be classified as a new and emerging form of international law known as transnational law.

Dr Tahmina Rashid

Dr Rashid is an Associate Professor in International Studies, Faculty of Arts and Design at the University of Canberra. She has a Master's Degree (Research) and PhD in Gender and Politics from the University of Melbourne. She has previously worked as the Program Director, International Development, RMIT University, and Assistant Professor in Pakistan. She was a Fulbright scholar in 1996 and was awarded the Asia Fellow Award, Ford Foundation in 2004–05 to work in the urban slums in Dhaka, Bangladesh. Her academic interests include feminist movements in South Asia; radical Islamic movements; urban/rural poverty; migration and identity; development and human rights; community sustainability and empowerment; and microcredit. Dr Rashid is the author of *Contested representations: Punjabi women in feminist debates in Pakistan*, Oxford University Press, 2006.

Dr Selver B. Sahin

Dr Sahin is a Research Fellow in the Global Cities Research Institute of RMIT University. Her research interests include perceptions of security in the post-Cold-War era, international intervention, and state building and national identity construction processes after conflict. In 2010 Dr Sahin published in *Asian Survey*, *Journal of Balkan and Near Eastern Studies* and *Southeast Asian Affairs*.